What Your Colleague

Smith and Imbrenda care about deep and meaningful learning. In this book, they show how argument can be taught in ways that develop tremendous engagement and deep understanding through a process that is in service of critical literacy and social imagination and responsibility. There are a lot of books about argument out there. I'd argue that this one is the best and most transformative I've ever read. The "so what" lessons on reasoning/warranting alone will transform your teaching of argument and of much else.

—Jeffrey D. Wilhelm, Distinguished Professor of English Education at
Boise State University, Author of *"You Gotta BE the Book!"* and
Diving Deep Into Nonfiction and 35 other books about literacy

I was impressed with how Smith and Imbrenda's approach helped students who are usually passive learners become so engaged in discussions about readings. Our test scores reflected that passion.

—Matthew Record, Principal, Pocomoke Middle School,
Pocomoke City, MD

In just a few weeks, Smith and Imbrenda's approach to instruction transformed my classroom. My students and I became passionate about our reading, writing, and discussions; our state assessment scores went up. This stuff works. I wish I had known about it my whole career.

—Hanna Poist, Language Arts Teacher, Pocomoke Middle School,
Pocomoke City, MD

Developing Writers of Argument is not only a practical guide for teaching students, but also a practical guide for educating teachers in the art of argument made simple. Instead of throwing the baby out with the bathwater, the authors draw upon years of research-based strategies and methodologies to make lessons real and relevant for today's learner. Reading the lessons provided me that "aha" moment and helped me to internalize the need for the three R's (relevance, responsibility, and respect) in teaching and learning.

—Kym Sheehan, Teacher/Curriculum Specialist,
Charlotte County Public Schools, FL

The lessons in this book are unique and engaging. My students can relate to the art of argument and have learned to respond using skills that have greatly enhanced their ability to express an argument persuasively. The ideas in this book have enabled a larger percentage of my students to write effectively and efficiently, and using them as a model has helped me design my own lessons that have proven equally effective. I highly recommend this writing program!

—Philadelphia Pathways Teacher

DEVELOPING
WRITERS *of*
ARGUMENT

To all of the students, teachers, student teachers, administrators, and colleagues who have made our work on the Pathways project so rewarding.

DEVELOPING WRITERS *of* ARGUMENT

TOOLS & RULES That Sharpen STUDENT REASONING

20 Ready-to-Use Lessons

 resources.corwin.com/writersofargument

Michael W. Smith
Jon-Philip Imbrenda
Foreword by Jim Burke

FOR INFORMATION:

Corwin
A SAGE Company
2455 Teller Road
Thousand Oaks, California 91320
(800) 233-9936
www.corwin.com

SAGE Publications Ltd.
1 Oliver's Yard
55 City Road
London EC1Y 1SP
United Kingdom

SAGE Publications India Pvt. Ltd.
B 1/I 1 Mohan Cooperative Industrial Area
Mathura Road, New Delhi 110 044
India

SAGE Publications Asia-Pacific Pte. Ltd.
3 Church Street
#10-04 Samsung Hub
Singapore 049483

Publisher and Senior Program Director: Lisa Luedeke
Editorial Development Manager: Julie Nemer
Editorial Assistants: Nicole Shade and Jessica Vidal
Production Editor: Melanie Birdsall
Copy Editor: Lana Arndt
Typesetter: C&M Digitals (P) Ltd.
Proofreader: Christine Dahlin
Indexer: Kathy Paparchontis
Cover and Interior Designer: Gail Buschman
Marketing Manager: Rebecca Eaton

Printed in the United States of America

ISBN 978-1-5063-5433-0

This book is printed on acid-free paper.

Certified Chain of Custody
Promoting Sustainable Forestry
www.sfiprogram.org
SFI-01268
SFI label applies to text stock

18 19 20 21 22 10 9 8 7 6 5 4 3 2 1

Contents

Visit the companion website at
resources.corwin.com/writersofargument
for downloadable lesson handouts.

Foreword

I learn something interesting, new, useful, and important every time I talk with Michael Smith, hear him speak at a conference, or read anything he writes. As with the best writers and thinkers, his ideas stem from careful and sustained attention, the results of which he has distilled down to their essence. As Michael said to me once when I expressed my frustration about the page limits imposed on a certain book I was writing, "Great! More thinking, less writing!" This passing remark sums up so much of the work Michael has done for so many years: a career spent thinking about the work we do every day as teachers with no greater aim than to help us do it a little better, a little deeper, a little more easily, so that we can enjoy the work and feel we have room to grow. These qualities are very much in evidence in the book you're holding, which Michael wrote with Jon-Philip Imbrenda, who, Michael told me, pushed him to do more and deeper thinking throughout their collaboration. Perhaps this newest book should be titled *Developing Teachers of Argument*.

While reading their work, I thought often of another book, Jack Schneider's *From the Ivory Tower to the Schoolhouse: How Scholarship Becomes Common Knowledge in Education*. In the book, Schneider identifies four "key characteristics" of scholarly work that achieves an enduring place in teachers' curriculum and, perhaps more important, their practice. All four of these characteristics are present in Michael and Jon-Philip's book and offer me what they would call a useful "frame" for discussing their ideas about argument.

First, according to Schneider, the ideas and the book that contains them must possess what he calls "perceived significance," which is another way of saying that the ideas offer a solution to something the reader sees as a real and pressing problem. Few subjects in recent years have presented more challenges to teachers than understanding and teaching students how to read for and write academic arguments. What Michael Smith and Jon-Philip Imbrenda do here is demystify not just argument but the larger subject of critical thinking and how they are related, why they matter, and, most important to our own work as teachers, how to teach them. Throughout this book, Michael and Jon-Philip "send a practitioner-friendly signal" (Schneider, 2014, p. 8) to their readers of the value and importance of critical thinking and argument, illustrating at every turn how to do or teach what they are discussing.

Schneider's second characteristic, "philosophical compatibility," suggests that for teachers to embrace and add some tool or technique to their practice, it must "clearly jibe with closely held beliefs" that validate what the teacher already knows and does, while promising to help them do it a little better. As I read this book, I felt at every turn as though I were reading about some aspect of what I already do, but I was learning new things—about argument, teaching, critical thinking, reading, and writing—that deepened my understanding and ability to teach these complex processes. This notion of philosophical compatibility is reflected in the "different set of three *R*'s" that Michael and Jon-Philip suggest should inform our classroom culture and practice: relevance, responsibility, and respect.

The third characteristic Schneider proposes is one all teachers value and which we often use to evaluate the ideas an author or presenter suggests we adopt; it is an idea Schneider calls "occupational realism" (p. 8). In short, it refers to the degree to which we can put another's ideas (in this case, the ideas from this book) into immediate use within the constraints of our teaching situation. So, for example, I necessarily read this book and wonder if the ideas would work in my classes of 35 seniors, whose abilities and needs stretch out across a pretty wide array, all of whom I must do my best to teach within our 51-minute periods and, when possible, while incorporating the computers we have in my classroom. Would the ideas here work just as well in a class that was 40 minutes or 90 minutes? Absolutely. Does one need a class set of Chromebooks to teach anything in this book? No, not at all. In other words, all the ideas I found here were realistic for me and any other teacher I know within the constraints of our teaching situation.

Finally, Schneider rounds out his list of characteristics of useful and enduring work by stressing the importance of what he calls "transportability." The typical teacher teaches more than one prep, grade level, or class, all of which make so many demands on the teacher that the teacher cannot often afford to invest the time it would take to learn a strategy or technique they can use in only one class or a few times a year. Transportability, in other words, refers to how well a tool, technique, or teaching strategy works across these different classes, throughout the year, or across the units one teaches in the course of a year. Here, again, Michael and Jon-Philip's ideas offer all of us useful resources we can use in August as well as April, in our freshman classes as well as in our AP English classes. Whether it is the templates or the idea of paragraph frames, the different types of analytical scales or the 20 different lessons themselves, the treasures in this book will spend as easily and well in one class as they will in another.

Schneider argues that if a book or theory has these four attributes I have outlined above in abundance, teachers will "notice, accept, use, and share it" with their colleagues and students (p. 7). Indeed, I find these attributes throughout this book, as I have in so much of the work Michael Smith has done over the years on his own, through his collaboration with Jeff Wilhelm, and now with Jon-Philip Imbrenda. So much of his work could be summed up in those four words above: he *notices* things he knows we want to learn or do better, frames them in language we can both *accept* and *use* in our own classrooms, and *shares it* with us in books like this that we cannot wait to share with our colleagues who are grappling with the same questions and challenges.

Whether you read this book for five minutes or five hours, you will find here the answers to questions you have asked about argument ("What is Toulmin's model of argument again?"), critical thinking ("How do you get students to think analytically about different types of literary and nonfiction texts?"), or instructional design ("How do you create a unit or a lesson about argument that students can grasp and apply to their own lives or the world at large?"). You will find here lessons for developing writers of argument, but you will also find this book is essential reading for developing teachers of argument.

—Jim Burke, Author of *Academic Moves for College and Career Readiness* and *The Common Core Companion*

Acknowledgments

In this book, we share the words of students who inspired and informed our teaching. IRB requirements keep us from mentioning them by name, but we owe them a debt of gratitude. Likewise, many thanks to their teacher and her principals, who also must remain nameless. Their openness to innovation, hospitality, and collaborative spirit have been crucial to the project's success. None of our work would have been possible without the support, financial and otherwise, of Chris Bruner, Dave Burkavage, Devin Cahill, Darin Hardy, Mike Shields, and all of their colleagues at Ernst & Young. Lisa Luedeke, our editor and the publisher at Corwin Literacy, helped us imagine the shape of the book and kept us on track as we worked to bring it to life. Julie Nemer, Nicole Shade, Melanie Birdsall, Gail Buschman, and the entire production and design team at Corwin have been a pleasure to work with. In addition, a team of teacher reviewers whom Corwin enlisted provided very valuable feedback as we were developing and refining our ideas. Hugh Kesson has been instrumental both in continuing the work of the Pathways program and in encouraging us to develop and refine our thinking.

Michael would also like to thank the late great George Hillocks, Jr., who taught him so much about teaching writing, and all of his University of Chicago friends with whom he has spent so many hours arguing about argument, especially Joe Flanagan, Steve Gevinson, Larry Johannessen, Betsy Kahn, Steve Littell, Tom McCann, and Peter Smagorinsky. Jeff Wilhelm is always a voice in Michael's ear when he thinks about teaching. Thanks also to Gregory M. Anderson, Michael's dean, who allowed him to carve out the time he needed to do the work we report here. Finally, thanks to his wife, Karen Flynn, for her ongoing encouragement to do the kind of work that matters in the lives of kids.

Jon-Philip adds his thanks to the faculty of the College of Education at Temple University who apprenticed him into the many conversations that have shaped his professional life: Carol Brandt, Wanda Brooks, Maia Cucchiara, Avi Kaplan, Kristie Newton, Frank Sullivan, and Barbara Wasik. He is also grateful for the advice and feedback, always apt and readily given, of Eli Goldblatt and George Newell. Above all, he thanks his family for their tireless optimism, encouragement, and support.

Publisher's Acknowledgments

Corwin gratefully acknowledges the following reviewers:

Lynn Angus Ramos
K–12 English Language Arts Coordinator
DeKalb County School District
Stone Mountain, GA

Andy Schoenborn
English Teacher
Mt. Pleasant Public Schools
Mt. Pleasant, MI

Lydia Bowden
Assistant Principal
Pinckneyville Middle School
Peachtree Corners, GA

Kym Sheehan
Teacher/Curriculum Specialist
Charlotte County Public Schools
Port Charlotte, FL

PART I

The Argument for Argument

Chapter 1

Introduction

In one of our favorite *Monty Python* skits, a man, played by Michael Palin, enters a clinic and explains to the receptionist that he would like to pay for a 5-minute argument. The receptionist directs him to a room down the hallway. When he enters the room, he finds another man, played by John Cleese, sitting at a desk.

"Ah, is this the right room for an argument?" Palin's character asks.

Cleese's character brusquely responds, "I've told you once."

"No, you haven't," says Palin.

"Yes, I have," replies Cleese.

The back and forth continues for a few more seconds as Palin's character becomes increasingly frustrated and eventually proclaims, "Look, this isn't an argument! It's just contradiction."

Cleese's character answers, "No, it isn't."

As the repartee continues, it evolves into an argument about the very definition of argument. Palin's character asserts, "An argument's not the same as contradiction."

Cleese's character rebuts, "Well, it can be."

"An argument is a connected series of statements to establish a definite proposition," Palin's character continues.

Cleese's character ripostes, "Look, if I argue with you, I must take up a contrary position."

Palin's character elaborates his position further. "Argument is an intellectual process. Contradiction is just the automatic gainsaying of anything the other person says."

Just as time runs out, Cleese's character offers up a final rebuttal, "No, it isn't."

We sometimes show this clip to our students and ask them to evaluate the quality of the argument that takes place between the two characters. Their responses vary, but for the most part what we find is that their understanding of argument is most closely reflected in the attitude of Cleese's character. They generally think of argument as an analog for debate or disagreement. While we certainly agree that debate and disagreement can sometimes be very effective classroom tools, we also try to honor the position that Palin's character emphasizes: Argument is not just debate and disagreement. It's a process—an intellectual process, a social process, a cultural process. Argument is reasoning. Argument is literacy.

> *Think of five different arguments you've seen on TV or in movies. You might consider legal arguments from courtroom dramas, political debates on news shows, family disputes on sitcoms, or disagreements among co-workers. How are arguments typically portrayed in popular culture? Do they reflect the points of view of both characters from the Monty Python skit?*
>
> **CONSIDER THIS**

Luckily, we're not alone in our appreciation for the value of argument. In recent years, literacy scholars have taken up the importance of argument as the basis for quality instruction in classrooms spanning grade levels and subject areas. Michael has previously written about the usefulness of argument as a way to address the Common Core State Standards for Language Arts (Smith, Wilhelm, & Fredricksen, 2012). Jon-Philip has designed and implemented an entire curriculum for college-bound high school students that is based on argument (Imbrenda, in press). Since the focus of this book is on providing teachers with ready-to-use lessons and activities, we're not going to get into a lengthy review of all the literature around the role of argument in secondary classrooms. Instead, we want to highlight and discuss briefly three primary reasons for teaching argument to all our students:

Argument is not just debate and disagreement.

Argument is reasoning. Argument is literacy.

1. Argument cultivates critical thinking.
2. Argument fosters collaborative reasoning.
3. Argument promotes a sense of social responsibility.

Let's think about each of these goals in a little more detail.

Argument Cultivates Critical Thinking

We make arguments every day of our lives. Whether we're choosing the best restaurant to eat at, the right smartphone to buy, or the podcasts we want to listen to on our commutes to work, we're taking into account many different factors and making a judgment based on how we evaluate those factors. We probably wouldn't refer to these everyday situations as examples of critical thinking. Most of the time these arguments take place internally, and the thought processes involved happen so fast we're barely aware of them.

Yet we probably all know a few people who seem to go a step further when it comes to certain kinds of everyday decisions. People who are very tech-savvy and carefully compare products based on complex hardware specifications. People who are particularly mindful of the nutritional quality of the foods they eat. People who are keenly discerning about the kinds of media they choose to consume. They're the people whom we go to for suggestions when we're not so sure what we want. Jon-Philip's brother, an engineer, spent nearly 2 months doing research before he purchased a new laptop. He compared dozens of pre-built models and even went a step further in comparing the specific components inside those pre-built models to decide if he wanted to go ahead and build one himself. His comparisons were richly informed by his expertise in the field of electrical engineering and by his understanding of the exact things he needed his laptop to be able to do effectively. We might be more inclined to refer to his decision-making process as an example of critical thinking because we have a clear sense of how his decision was influenced by information available to him and the deep knowledge needed to understand and interpret that information. In fact, part of what makes so-called critical thinking different from just plain old thinking is that critical thinking requires that we have some degree of awareness of what's happening when we make decisions, consider evidence, generate interpretations, and act upon our judgments. Critical thinking is about getting beyond "Here's what I think," and into the realm of "Here's what I think. Here's what makes me think that. And here's why it matters." In this respect, we agree with Michael's mentor, George Hillocks, when he argues that the kind of critical thinking we often champion as an essential goal of education is, in fact, sound argumentation (Hillocks, 2010). Simply put, thinking critically and arguing effectively are the same thing!

When we shift the focus of our instruction onto argumentation through lessons like the ones in this book, and give our students frequent opportunities to build arguments across a variety of situations, we're cultivating the kind of explicit awareness of their own thinking that characterizes Jon-Philip's brother's meticulous efforts to select the best laptop computer. We're helping them to move beyond their tacit judgments and into the deeper and often much more complex inner workings of those judgments. If we do so over time, we help our students become flexible and strategic in their academic lives. This kind of thinking becomes a habit, and with encouragement, they are able to transfer their new skills to the reading, writing, and range of other tasks they are frequently expected to carry out for school. We hope that the lessons and tools we present in this book will serve as good examples of how argumentation cultivates the kind of critical thinking we want our students to engage in on a regular basis in our classrooms—and will provide practice for your students to do the same. Our lessons are designed to teach students to carefully consider the knowledge and information available to them, while providing them with questions that are relevant to their lives both inside and outside of the classroom.

Argument Fosters Collaborative Reasoning

Much of what we just discussed in the previous section reflects fairly common understandings about the value of argument as in the development of individual learners. However, an equally valuable yet frequently overlooked aspect of argumentation is its inherently social nature. Newell and his colleagues (2011) proclaim the benefits of argument as a social practice carried out by groups of people across many different contexts as opposed to viewing it only as a reflection of an individual's cognitive ability. Such benefits are particularly important for us as educators to understand, as research has shown that the kinds of collaborative reasoning that characterize socially directed arguments can become powerful contributors to deep and meaningful learning (Clark et al., 2003; Nussbaum, 2008). Recognizing argument as a social practice helps us get beyond debate and disagreement and into the kinds of collaborative conversations that impact the world in important ways.

As a social practice, argument is paramount to the cooperative efforts of professionals in many fields. For example, Hagler and Brem (2008) examined the ways that professional nurses in critical care environments relied on argumentative reasoning to provide care for people with very serious medical conditions. Through ongoing series of polite informal exchanges of both information and interpretations of that information, nurses were able to combine their knowledge and expertise when reaching agreements about how to handle specific patients. This study is but one of many instances in which argumentative reasoning is shown to be central to the kinds of collaboration involved in people's professional lives.

Moreover, evidence has shown that students who participate consistently in collaborative arguments in the classroom can develop powerful habits of reasoning as they adopt the successful strategies of their peers (Clark et al., 2003). Students who struggled to generate effective arguments on their own showed tremendous improvement once argument was placed in the forefront of the social activity in the classroom. Much as the nurses in the critical care centers, students in classrooms became active participants in their own learning as they worked together to reach agreements. Due to its inherently social nature, argument bridges the

> Research has shown that the kinds of collaborative reasoning that characterize socially directed arguments can become powerful contributors to deep and meaningful learning.

important divide between the individual learner and the social dynamic of the classroom. We hope that the tools and lessons we present in this book will serve as good examples of how placing argument at the center of instruction can transform a classroom dynamic into one that is rich with talk and other forms of cooperative activity.

CONSIDER THIS

Can you think of a recent experience where you and one or more colleagues had to "argue" to come to a consensus around an important issue in your school? Did you think of what you were doing as an argument? Was the discussion ultimately beneficial?

Argument Promotes a Sense of Social Responsibility

In January of 2015 the Pew Research Center published a report on the findings from a study in which they examined Americans' attitudes toward the importance of science and the value of scientific findings (Kennedy & Funk, 2015). They administered surveys to a representative sample of 2,002 adults and compared their responses to the responses of 3,748 members of the American Association for the Advancement of Science (AAAS). What the report found is somewhat alarming: While Americans largely value the importance of science and believe that scientific endeavors should be funded by the government, they are far less likely to embrace the understandings that scientific research generates. For example, despite the fact that 88% of the AAAS scientists reported that genetically modified foods are safe to eat, 57% of the American public reported that they believed genetically modified foods to be unsafe to eat. In short, Americans like the idea of science, but they seem less willing to take scientific research into consideration when it conflicts with their personal values and lifestyle choices.

Why do we care about these findings, and what do they have to do with argument? Well, we're concerned that studies such as this reflect a cultural phenomenon that is dangerous for our students. Large-scale efforts to evaluate students' reading and writing have consistently shown that students at all grade levels struggle to reason carefully from evidence and data (National Center for Education Statistics [NCES], 2012). Consistent with the implications of the Pew study, our students seem to be drifting into a malaise of anti-intellectualism and unwillingness to engage deeply and critically with the world around them. In an era where people have unprecedented access to information, our culture seems to be more willing than ever to remain complacent in its often-misguided assumptions.

If we view this as a strictly academic problem, then the previous two sections should hint at how argument can address that problem. But we don't view it as a strictly academic problem. We view it as a social problem, though it's a problem that involves education. Yet reform efforts such as the Common Core and other state standards seem to have no explicit interest in confronting this social problem. The majority of standards focus on college and career readiness. But what about readiness for responsible citizenship? What about fostering the social conscience needed to assume important roles in the future of America? As educators, we're very much concerned with not just the colleges and careers our students matriculate into, but also with the kinds of people they become. We hope that the lessons and tools we provide in this book will demonstrate how our emphasis on argument also contributes to how students read and respond to the world around them, and how they develop identities as responsible members of society.

> *Recently, concerns around the increase in so-called fake news have begun to permeate our classrooms. How do you help your students navigate the wealth of media that surround them? Can you think of a recent experience with a student or colleague that gave you some concern for how people determine what is truthful or accurate?*

CONSIDER THIS

What This Book Can Offer

The chapters ahead are intended to serve as a resource for teachers who want to introduce argument into their classrooms. Chapter 2 provides a brief overview of the framework that guides our instructional approach and an explanation of a model of argument that has proved useful to us in our classrooms. In Chapter 3, we give detailed explanations of a few specific instructional tools that we have had great success with in helping students to approach reading, writing, and talking argumentatively.

Chapters 4–7 provide 20 ready-to-go, stand-alone lessons. Each chapter focuses on a different kind of lesson. Chapter 4 shares six lessons designed to introduce the model of argumentation by engaging in everyday arguments. Chapter 5 presents six lessons that focus more precisely on the three elements of that model. Chapter 6 comprises six lessons that focus in some way or another on textual analysis. Chapter 7 presents two lessons that require students to apply what they've learned to important life decisions.

We chose our lessons for a number of reasons:

- They illustrate a wide range of topics that promote argumentation.

- They demonstrate different ways of using some of our tools.

- They can stand as the basis for entire units or fit snugly into pre-existing units.

- They feature an array of different types of data from which arguments can be generated.

- They represent a diversity of argumentative contexts and situations.

As educators who have worked in many different environments, we deeply appreciate the many significant variations that characterize different classrooms, regions, school systems, and pedagogical approaches. With this in mind, we've also designed our lessons using a flexible format. While we will give suggestions as to how a teacher might want to implement our topics and tools, there is also a great deal of room for individual variation. Our lessons and tools can accommodate many different formats—full class, small group, peer-to-peer—as well as mediums for communication—talking, formal and informal writing, visual and multimedia presentations, etc. We want our materials to be as adaptable as possible.

Each lesson also includes examples of student writing we've collected through our work in a comprehensive urban high school. As you'll see, our students, like many in America, struggle with the complex kinds of reasoning we ask them to carry out, and with the many challenges that come with trying to communicate their ideas in writing. We chose the student work here not because it was representative of the "best," but because it was representative of the range of students' struggles with the demands we placed on them and the high expectations to which we held them. Therefore, we've also included examples of how we might respond to each student's work in the hope that our efforts will prove insightful to teachers who will likely find that their students experience very similar struggles. And perhaps more importantly, we've added a few notes to make visible our own reasoning as educators who want to reflect on and improve our practice in response to the emergent needs of our students. We think of this as an example of how data can be used to drive instruction—a distinct kind of argumentative reasoning in itself!

Although the 20 lessons that we share provide a clear illustration of our approach and although we think that you could use them effectively with your students, we realize that 20 lessons do not a curriculum make. We'll close, therefore, with a brief discussion about how you might use the lessons as your year goes on.

Notes

Chapter 2

A Classroom Culture of Argumentation

Revisiting the Three *R*'s

In the previous chapter, we outlined three primary reasons we believe argument should be taught to all our students:

1. Argument cultivates critical thinking.

2. Argument fosters collaborative reasoning.

3. Argument promotes a sense of social responsibility.

Here we want to give a clear account of how we see these things at work inside our classrooms. Consider the following scenario:

Over the past few weeks, students have been reading *The Kite Runner* (Hosseini, 2003) and considering the question "To what extent am I responsible to others?" To accompany their readings of the novel, they have also been reading about people whose lives raise interesting questions about the extent of our personal responsibilities. One such person is Pat Tillman, an all-pro safety for the Arizona Cardinals who, just after the events of September 11, 2001, abandoned his NFL career to enlist in the army. Tragically, Tillman was killed in Afghanistan 2 years later. Tillman's life introduces some really powerful questions around the extent to which a person is responsible: Was Tillman's decision to join the army an example of noble sacrifice, or reckless idealism? To examine this question, students read two short editorials offering contrasting views of Tillman's life. They also read a short news article reporting on some of the controversy around his death. The news report included testimony from his bereaved loved ones.

In class, the students are discussing their responses to the set of readings. The conversation goes something like this:

Teacher: Okay, so we've been reading some about Pat Tillman, and it's pretty clear that people have different positions on him. Where do you stand?

Student 1: I think Tillman was a hero.

Teacher:	Okay, well, what makes you say so?
Student 1:	He gave his life for his country.
Teacher:	Right. But so what?
Student 1:	The author here gives the dictionary definition of what hero means. Tillman is definitely a hero because he fits the definition.
Student 2:	I don't agree. All he did was hurt the people who matter most to him.
Teacher:	Hmmm, that's interesting. What makes you say so?
Student 2:	You can read right here how his mom and his brother feel like he died for no reason.
Teacher:	Of course his family was devastated by the loss. But so what?
Student 2:	Well he was responsible to them, too. He wasn't thinking about them when he joined up to fight. You can't be a respectable or responsible or heroic person if you don't care about the people closest to you.
Student 3:	And what about all of his fans from the NFL? He was already a role model to many people, a lot of them probably kids.
Teacher:	What makes you say so?
Student 3:	Well, you know how fans feel about sporting figures.
Teacher:	Nope. I'm not much of a sports fan.
Student 3:	Just look at the article. It says in the article that he turned down an offer from the Rams just to stay with the Cardinals.
Teacher:	Right, he did. So what?
Student 3:	Well that means he must have really loved his fans, and he didn't want to let them down.

You can probably imagine how this discussion could proceed from here. Students 1, 2, and 3 could continue to press their positions. Other students could join in to defend or refute any of those positions. Or another student could propose an alternative, equally viable way of thinking about the extent of Tillman's responsibility. Of course, at some point, we might try to steer the discussion back to the novel the students have been reading, since it also offers a range of perspectives regarding the extent of the characters' responsibilities. Even though the characters in the novel may face different circumstances than Tillman faced, the dimensions of the question are still the same: Are we most responsible to our close loved ones? To our local communities? To our nation? To all people? Or perhaps we're most responsible only to ourselves?

The argument taking place in this scenario is clearly not of the yes-or-no variety so poignantly satirized by the *Monty Python* crew. There is no winner or loser. There is no obvious right or wrong position. Yet the conversation taking place meets our criteria for the kind of learning we want to promote in our classrooms. We're sure you're familiar with the age-old three *R*'s of school. Well, we like to think about our classrooms in terms of a different set of *R*'s: *Relevance*, *Responsibility*, and *Respect*. Let's talk about how each of these *R*'s is evidenced in the scenario above:

> We like to think about our classrooms in terms of a different set of *R*'s: *Relevance, Responsibility,* and *Respect.*

- **Relevance:** Students in our classrooms are hardly surprised when we ask them to read things. The problem is, they don't often see how the things they have to read are relevant to their lives, both now and in the future. We confront this problem head-on by treating the texts students read as turns in an ongoing conversation. Moreover, we make sure those conversations involve topics and themes that are important to adolescents who are at a stage in their lives where they must confront many different existential issues. For example, by using the question "To what extent am I responsible to others?" as a staging ground that unites the things they read into an ongoing conversation, students can see how the things they do in school are connected to their immediate lives. Furthermore, they are also practicing with the kinds of reasoning and problem-solving that will aid them in their futures both in and out of the classroom.

- **Responsibility:** When students understand how the things they do in class are relevant to their immediate lives and their futures, they start to participate in their schooling in new ways. These new ways of participation involve developing a sense of responsibility toward both the quality of their arguments, as well as to the moral and ethical subtexts of the things we ask them to generate arguments around. For example, by examining the life of Pat Tillman in the context of the question "To what extent am I responsible to others?" the students begin to understand how they are accountable for supporting their positions through specific forms of reasoning. Expectations for what counts as a good argument become the shared responsibility of the entire classroom. Moreover, the positions they generate are also reflections of their own existential growth—they are giving deep consideration to how they, too, must become responsible participants within many domains of their lives: home, school, workplace, community, and so forth.

- **Respect:** Assuming the responsibilities that come with being a relevant participant in classroom conversations requires that students become careful readers, active listeners, and conscientious contributors to the ongoing spoken and written dialogue around them. The classroom is no longer a collection of individual learners; rather, it is a community of aspiring intellectuals who are preparing to enter into the larger conversations of their lives. Through this preparation, students develop a deep sense of respect for others, for the need to ascertain the quality of the messages conveyed to them through peers and popular media, and for the ways in which their roles as classroom participants both shape and are shaped by the ways in which they are able to participate in the classroom community. In short, they are not just learning *what* they need to know, but they are also learning *how* to contribute to the generation of knowledge. This kind of learning, we believe, engenders a considerable degree of respect.

Conversation as a Metaphor for Learning

By now, you've probably noticed that our view of learning is firmly rooted in a particular metaphor: We see learning as participating in a series of ongoing conversations. At times these conversations are spoken. At times they're written. At times they are carried out through a wide range of media and modes of expression. And at times they're entirely internal—they are the conversations we have within ourselves that Vygotsky (1987), one of our intellectual heroes, so focused on in his extremely influential work. Sometimes these conversations are situated within a particular domain as when we learn about cells in biology class, or when we study chains of events from U.S. history; at other times, they cut across domains as when we examine the impact of carbon monoxide on the atmosphere, or when we try to unravel the complex phenomenon of human intelligence. In all cases, learning is about becoming a more and more capable participant in an ever-expanding variety of conversations.

> We see learning as participating in a series of ongoing conversations.

Think about five different conversations you've participated in over the last week. Perhaps you browsed the news online before work, discussed dinner options with a spouse or partner, exchanged lesson ideas with a colleague, read a few chapters from a novel before bedtime, etc. What kinds of knowledge and experiences informed your capacity to participate in each of these conversations? How were they similar or different?

CONSIDER THIS

As much as we would like to lay claim to the conversation metaphor, admittedly, it is not our own. It is borne out of our appreciation for some of our most important intellectual influences—appreciation we developed through the conversations we participate in. As we mentioned above, it is rooted in the work of Vygotsky (1987), who first theorized the extent to which learning was a function of our social encounters as opposed to innate cognitive processes. It is rooted in the work of Jean Lave and Etienne Wenger (1991), an unlikely duo (Lave is a social anthropologist, and Wenger is a computer scientist!) who studied how people learn in a wide range of informal contexts to show how learning is deeply situated in our immediate contexts and interactions with others. And, of course, we have to give credit to Arthur Applebee (1996, p. 3) who so eloquently argues for a vision of curriculum as "knowledge-in-action," arising out of "participation in ongoing conversations about things that matter."

Such conversations, when held to Applebee's vision, are powerful both within and across classrooms and other settings. Above, we used the example of "To what extent am I responsible to others?" as a way to unify the things students do in class under a common purpose that promotes relevance, responsibility, and respect. Think about how that conversation could carry into a social studies classroom where students are learning about the central tenets of democracy, or a science classroom where students are learning about the impact of pollution on the regional ecology. And beyond the classroom, the conversations will surely carry into our students' lives when they are ready to vote in local and national elections or make informed decisions about their career paths.

CONSIDER THIS

Another favorite unit of ours is built around the question "What does it mean to be smart?" What kinds of cross-curricular connections can you think of that this unit would benefit from? In what ways do you think participating in the conversation around that question would aid students outside of school?

Staging Conversations in Your Classroom

Embracing the conversation metaphor so as to establish relevance, responsibility, and respect as the governing principles in the classroom allows for argumentation to become the basis for how shared purposes and understandings are negotiated by the students themselves. Argumentation becomes a distinct kind of social activity—a collective set of practices that allow for conversations to be carried out on a daily basis. Setting the stage for these conversations is not as difficult as it may seem. It does require some planning, but it is also a function of how we frame and present things to our students.

Let's take a very prototypical example: reading *Romeo and Juliet* with a group of ninth graders who are dealing with the transition into high school. Consider three possible prompts that could invite reflection and discussion, both oral and written, once students have completed their readings of the play:

1. Explain how the prologue of *Romeo and Juliet* sets up the ending of the play.

2. To what extent does Romeo and Juliet's relationship resemble other relationships that you've experienced, seen, or read about?

3. Which of the three works we've read—*Romeo and Juliet, Oedipus the King,* or *The Crucible*—most effectively responds to the question "To what extent can we control our own destiny?"

We would argue that, as the basis for promoting a culture of conversation, these three prompts do not work equally well. Let's consider each one:

- **Prompt 1:** The prologue of *Romeo and Juliet,* while an excellent example of Shakespeare's stylistic acumen, is rather straightforward insofar as it prepares the audience for the ending of the play. We're told that amidst the feuding between two noble families, a pair of young lovers will enter into an ill-fated affair that will end in their deaths. There's not much subtlety or ambiguity here. The first prompt gives students very few options for developing a sustainable interpretation. In fact, if we think about it, the first prompt calls for little more than a perfunctory summary of the plot of the play. Don't get us wrong: the reasons that teachers might cite for favoring the first prompt are usually quite valid. They want to make sure their assignments have clear expectations that can be fairly assessed. They look at that first prompt, and they see something that is easy to manage, while still placing appropriate demands on their students. We respect their concerns, but we're far less willing to settle for the kinds of conversations that prompt could generate.

- **Prompt 2:** This one is definitely a step in the right direction. It has some good potential to invite ongoing conversations within culturally relevant domains. However, when we think about it in terms of a conversation that can unfold according to shared practices and understandings, we're a little less enthusiastic. We appreciate the range and variety of responses it could elicit from our students, and we like how an important work of literature stands at the center of the conversation, but we don't see many opportunities to shape those responses into academically sanctioned arguments. The problem is that the question of whether or not *Romeo and Juliet* exemplifies other kinds of relationships doesn't reflect the kinds of questions that are taken up in the communities of practice we're preparing our students to enter. Except for some very specialized sub-fields in philosophy or anthropology, we're not aware of any disciplines that have developed agreed-upon ways to investigate that question. We wouldn't really know how to shape our students' responses into academically sanctioned modes of reasoning and forms of communication. Although the question certainly calls for an argument, it's not quite the kind of argument we want to apprentice them into. So, while we would endorse asking Question 2, we don't think a steady diet of Question 2's provides the kind of practice students need to become relevant participants in a wide range of conversations both inside and outside of school.

- **Prompt 3:** This one calls for the right kind of argument. First, it is framed in the context of a broad question that has existential value to our students (and to us, for that matter!). Second, it involves multiple texts, and each of those texts offers a different commentary on the question. Third, it invites many possibilities for sustainable responses. Fourth, to develop an effective argument in response to the prompt, our students will have to practice argumentative strategies that are common across many academic disciplines. The prompt initiates a turn in an ongoing conversation within a culturally relevant domain, and that domain is one in which there are agreed-upon ways of reasoning and modes of communication. The prompt provides our students with an opportunity to participate legitimately in the activity of classroom life. We can work backward from that prompt and prepare our students to take it on by providing them with clear strategies and opportunities to practice those strategies. In short, it reflects a classroom approach guided by conversation in which argument is central to how that conversation is carried out.

CONSIDER THIS

Take a look at a couple of your most recent writing prompts. Which one works best as the basis for promoting a culture of conversation?

So What, Exactly, Is an Argument, Anyway?

Both of us come from, shall we say, boisterous households in which arguments bear greater resemblance to the *Monty Python* skit than they do to the kind of reasoned written or oral argumentation we want our students to be able to engage in. Michael's mom, for instance, was known to say, "You can't care about your side as much as I care about mine because you never yell." We suspect that the same is true for many of our students. And the airwaves are full of shows, be they focused on sports or politics, in which bombast rather than reasoning is the order of the day. So, we have to help our students understand that academic argumentation requires something else of them. We have found that the thinking of Stephen Toulmin helps us do just that.

Unlike the classical rhetoricians before him, whose interest in argument was focused on the formal logic used to ascertain universal principles, Toulmin's (1958) work looked closely at the kinds of arguments that actually happen in the world. He analyzed arguments across many different settings—from highly formal courts of law right down to everyday arguments around the dinner table—and compared these different arguments in order to describe elements that were universal to all of them. We're going to focus on just a few of those elements here as we have found that they give us what we need for our classrooms without letting things get too complicated.

Claims

According to Toulmin's model, the origin point for an argument can be traced back to one or more *claims*. A claim is a position a person asserts and expects to be accepted on its merit. Claims come in many varieties. Oftentimes they are statements of agreement or disagreement. Someone may disagree with a certain new policy that has been implemented in their workplace, for example. Claims assert a position with respect to the immediate circumstances in which an argument is taking place. As you saw in the classroom conversation we shared at the beginning of this chapter, when we prompt our students to generate claims, we ask, "Where do you stand?"

In order for a claim to be effective, it has to be both debatable and defensible. A claim is hardly worth supporting if no reasonable person would object to its merit. Nor is it worth asserting a claim if it can't reasonably be supported. The reason we selected Pat Tillman as a case for our students to consider is that we found such divided opinions about him. If everyone agreed that Tillman was a hero, there would be no need to support that argument. After making that claim, Student 1 would be greeted with nods rather than questions that called for her to spin out her reasoning.

We think this is an important quality of claims to understand because it contributes heavily to our thinking when we're designing our lessons and activities. We want to make sure we're giving our students materials that invite them to develop effective claims that demand careful support. All too often we see students making arguments around claims that aren't both debatable and defensible. No one would disagree that Harper Lee portrays a prejudiced society in *To Kill a Mockingbird*, yet we've seen students compose entire essays around such a claim. At the same time, there is simply no way to defend the claim that Bob Ewell really did die by falling on his knife. But the claim "Our readings on social change convince me that Harper Lee is wrong in suggesting that lasting social change has to come very slowly" provides the grist for an essay that will both require and allow a writer to fully develop his or her argument.

> In order for a claim to be effective, it has to be both debatable and defensible.

Data

If claims form the basis of an argument, what forms the basis of a claim? The answer, according to Toulmin, is *data*. Data refers broadly to the knowledge and experience that we appeal to as the foundation for a claim. It answers the question "What makes you say so?" or "What have you got to go on?" In conventional use, the term data conjures up images of spreadsheets and binary code, but the way we use the term here includes much more than empirical measurements or statistical formulations. Many things can count as data depending on the context of an argument. In the Tillman example, students drew on evidence from the texts that the class read. Imagine a unit focused on the question "What makes a good teacher?" If a student made the claim that "The most important characteristic of a good teacher is content knowledge," he or she might turn to findings from research on effective teaching. If a student made the claim that "the most important characteristic of a good teacher is being caring" he or she might share an anecdote about how a caring teacher improved his or her achievement in a difficult subject area.

What's crucially important to understand is that data have to form a safe starting point to support a claim. If the audience for an argument is not willing to stipulate to the data, there is no sense advancing the argument any further. In fact, if the audience is not willing to stipulate to the data, the data are really a claim.

Let's turn once again to the argument at the beginning of the chapter. Student 1 defends her claim that Tillman was a hero by offering a fact that's beyond dispute ("He gave his life for his country"). Student 2, on the other hand begins his argument with this statement: "All he did was hurt the people who matter most to him." The teacher is not willing to stipulate to that datum and so says, "Hmmm, that's interesting. What makes you say so?" Only when Student 2 says, "You can read right here how his mom and his brother feel like he died for no reason" does the argument move beyond a demand for data.

Warrants

We've discussed how claims have to be both debatable and defensible, and we demonstrated how data have to provide a safe starting point to support those claims. But effective arguments also require the audience or interlocutor to accept the bigger assumptions underlying our claims and data. Toulmin (1958) calls those assumptions *warrants*. Warrants are perhaps the most novel contribution of Toulmin's model for argument, and they're also one of the trickier concepts to grasp. A warrant is a general rule or principle that authorizes someone to move from data to a claim or claims. In everyday situations, warrants are often tacit. For example, when we choose a television show to watch among the many options available, we're probably not going to elaborate on the reasons for our selection. We know what we like. However, if we're trying to convince a friend to watch a show, we're probably going to supply some data—we might tell her that the show is historically accurate, or that it features a favorite actor of hers. Those data will make our case more convincing *only* if they match with her personal criteria for what makes a good television show. If our friend responds by saying, "Well, I learn enough about history from the books I read so I prefer my television shows to take me out of the real world!" our argument is ineffective not because of the claim or the data, but because of disagreement over the warrant at play.

Student 2 in our sample argument at the beginning of the chapter provides an excellent illustration when he says, "You can't be a respectable or responsible or heroic person if you don't care about the people closest to you." He explicitly states a general rule that connects his data to his claim.

Public policy debates provide a great illustration of the importance of warrants. As we write this paragraph, debate rages on over the American Health Care

Act (AHCA), the proposed Republican replacement for President Obama's Affordable Care Act. Proponents of this act point to the fact that it eliminates the individual mandate. That fact is beyond dispute, but it only matters if you share proponents' belief that ensuring freedom of choice is an essential element of legislation. On the other hand, opponents of the American Health Care Act point to the fact that the Congressional Budget Office's analysis has it that the AHCA would insure 14 million fewer Americans. But if you accept that fact, it only matters if you agree that health care is a right that the government needs to insure.

Take a look at a current public policy debate. Examine the claims and sub-claims of that debate. What kinds of data do proponents and opponents draw upon? Consider whether they articulate the underlying principles (warrants) that inform their selection of data. How were the proponents' arguments similar? How are they different?

CONSIDER THIS

We want our students to be able to engage the arguments that matter most in their homes, schools, and communities. And we want them to engage in those arguments in ways that will prompt them to think differently, to challenge their own assumptions, and to appreciate the view of someone whose assumptions may be different than theirs. Our hope is that this book will provide you with some tools to foster a similar appreciation for arguments among your students. It is to a description of those tools that we now turn.

Chapter 3

Our Instructional Approach

Simply being able to articulate the target of our teaching pales in comparison to the difficulty of hitting that target.

In Chapter 1, we talked about why we value the teaching of argument. In Chapter 2, we offered conversation as a metaphor for the kind of learning we try to foster, and we detailed the elements of the kind of arguments we try to generate through conversations in and across settings. But simply being able to articulate the target of our teaching pales in comparison to the difficulty of hitting that target. That's why the rest of this book will focus on what we think are transferable tools that will help you enact classroom conversations that will apprentice students into being able to employ the elements of Toulmin's model effectively.

Transferable Classroom Tools

Indeed, our work in Chapter 2 introduced the first of those tools: the questions derived from Stephen Toulmin's discussion of the essential elements of argument. We think those questions are very useful tools, in part because questions are one of the primary methods of instruction ELA teachers employ, so using them doesn't require significant changes to teachers' practice. These questions demonstrate how questions relate to Toulmin's model:

- A *claim* is the answer to the question "Where do you stand?"

- *Data* are the answer to the question "What makes you say so?"

- *Warrants* are the answer to the question "So what?"

Stein and Albro (2001) note that children as young as 3 can produce all of the elements of an effective argument in interaction with a conversational partner. Of course, in writing, there is no conversational partner. That's why we continually repeat the Toulmin questions in our classrooms in the hope that our students will internalize them, becoming, in effect, their own conversational partner as they write. The questions also help our students understand and operationalize the elements of Toulmin's model. Indeed, our students regularly refer to their data as "What makes you say so?" and their warrants as "So whats?" We establish the notion of data as a safe starting point by illustrating it through classroom conversations. Data that are safe earn a "So what?" from us. Data that aren't safe act as claims, so they get another "What makes you say so?"

As you'll see in the lessons we will soon be presenting, we introduce the elements of argument by engaging students in the kind of everyday arguments kids are likely to have as a matter of course in their daily lives. Consider, for example, this discussion of whether someone looking for a phone should buy Apple or Android.

Student: People looking for phones should buy Apple!

Teacher: What makes you say so?

Student: They're the coolest.

Teacher: What makes you say so?

Student: People wait in line to buy them.

Teacher: So what?

Student: So that means they're popular.

Teacher: So what?

Student: Well, if they're popular, they must be good.

As you can see, the repeated "What makes you say so?" cues the student that the teacher would not stipulate to the data provided. Once the data were safe, the teacher cued the need for the warrant with a "So what?"

> *Do you have any specific phrases or questions you like to use to prompt students to talk in your classroom?*
>
> **CONSIDER THIS**

Essential/Enduring Questions

If you want to make argument central to your work with students, you have to create a context that supports it. In our view, the best way to do so is to structure your instruction in units that are built around essential (Michael's preferred term) or enduring (Jon-Philip's preference) questions. (We'll use EQ to refer to these questions through the rest of the book. You can choose which E you prefer.) EQs are questions of deep personal or social importance, the kind of questions you discussed long into the night during your first year of college. Most English teachers we know came to the profession at least in part because their reading (and sometimes writing) helped them think about those questions. We're talking about questions like "What makes me me?" or "Do people get what they deserve?" They're the kind of questions that people have been talking about for years, generations, even epochs.

By their very nature, EQs are complex and unsettled. Multiple positions in response to them are sustainable. Multiple kinds of data can be offered to support those positions. The general rules that link the data and claims can come from a variety of domains. EQs, therefore, provide the perfect context in which to teach argument.

We worked together at a neighborhood high school here in Philadelphia in the Pathways Project, a Temple College of Education initiative supported by Ernst & Young, whose goal is to better prepare students for the rigors of college reading and writing. (The Pathways Project also has a quantitative reasoning component.) The curriculum we devised is built around EQs. We developed the questions in three primary ways.

1. We developed some EQs because the questions are ones we wanted our students to think about. As we were beginning our initial planning, we read an article in the *New York Times Magazine* titled "Who Gets to Graduate?" which details the success the University of Texas had improving the persistence of first-generation college students by making a part of students' first-year orientation a short online program designed to challenge the entity view of intelligence, that is that intelligence is simply a trait one is born with as opposed to one that's affected by a person's behavior. So, the first EQ we asked is, "What does it mean to be smart?"

2. We developed some EQs because they mapped on to reading or writing we wanted students to do. The teacher with whom we worked wanted students to read *The Kite Runner*, so we asked, "To what extent are people responsible for each other?," the primary question we think animates that book. For a unit on the writing of college essays, we used the EQ, "What makes me *me*?"

3. We developed other EQs by paying attention to issues and ideas we heard students talking about. It didn't take us long to realize just how important music is to the students we were working with, so we asked, "On balance, has hip-hop had a positive or negative effect on American society?" All of these questions were able to sustain students' interest for weeks of ongoing argument-centered conversation.

In order to make sure that those conversations stayed focused, we thought through the dimensions of each of the questions. For example, we took up the question "What does it really mean to be smart?" by asking two subquestions:

"Where can the causes of smartness be found?"

"How is smartness manifested?"

Then we selected texts that answered those questions in different ways. The following outline illustrates the planning we did for the smartness unit. Using the readings, we determined possible positions to help give students a safe starting point.

UNIT: What does it mean to be smart?

SUBQUESTION: Where does intelligence come from?

- Position #1: Intelligence is an innate or genetic construct.

- Position #2: Intelligence is a product of individual agency, determination, and willfulness.

- Position #3: Intelligence is a social construct that reflects the values of dominant groups.

SUBQUESTION: How does intelligence manifest?

- Position #1: Intelligence is best understood as a function of how successful a person is with traditional academic subjects such as reading, writing, and math.

- Position #2: Intelligence is a reflection of how skilled or talented a person is within a particular domain.

- Position #3: Intelligence is a function of how resourceful a person is, how well a person can interact with others, and how well a person can solve practical problems.

Thinking through the question and subquestions in this way guaranteed that we could have focused conversations about questions to which there were no easy answers. Our students had to understand that whatever positions they ended up taking would have to be defended.

Can you think of any EQs you might like to use to organize ongoing conversations in your classroom?

CONSIDER THIS

Gateway Activities

Another tool we use is what Hillocks (1995, p. 166) calls gateway activities. Hillocks notes that gateway activities for the teaching of argument require a dataset "in which a problem lurks" and in which students will take an immediate interest. As you'll see, some of our datasets involve comparisons of products/services that kids care about. Others relate to life choices they'll soon be facing. Still others are sets of scenarios we've designed ourselves to give visibility to the problems that often lurk inside conventional attitudes toward things like intelligence and responsibility. Lessons 11 and 13 in this book provide examples of these problematic scenario sets.

These scenarios are especially useful for introducing EQs. We try to make them complex. They're of little use if every student would rank them in the same way. When rankings are different, discussion ensues, providing the opportunity not only for students to begin thinking about the dimensions of the EQ, but also for the teacher to employ the Toulmin questions to help students produce the elements of effective argumentation.

Gateway activities for the teaching of argument require a dataset "in which a problem lurks" and in which students will take an immediate interest.

Semantic Differential Scales

Another tool we employ is the semantic differential scale (SDS). SDSs were developed by a group of educational psychologists led by Charles Osgood as a way to measure how people make meaning (Osgood, Suci, & Tannenbaum, 1957). At the time, it was already understood that language was central to meaning-making, but researchers were not always able to get at the full complexity of the processes by which meaning is made. Such research tended to focus on typical patterns of language use rather than variations across individuals. So the SDS was used as a tool to allow for researchers to capture the wide variations across individuals and groups in how meaning was made. We use the tool similarly to help our students make meaning out of the things we present to them.

An SDS is a scale that positions words or phrases in bipolar relationships. To illustrate its use as an instructional tool, consider the following scenario:

A student is asked to respond to an argumentative text. The text presents an author's case for "the most intellectual rapper" and also includes excerpted song lyrics from the rapper's work. After reading the text, the student begins by marking the "6" on the following scale in response to the quality of the author's argument:

Once the student has marked the scale, the student has, in fact, made a claim, so the teacher can employ the Toulmin probes to help the student develop the underlying reasoning behind that claim. The conversation then might go something like this:

Teacher: Okay, so where do you stand?

Student: I marked a 6.

Teacher: A 6 is pretty close to unconvincing. What makes you say so?

Student: Here in the lyrics are a bunch of words that I don't even know what they mean. Words like "celestial," "diasporic," and "consciousness."

Teacher: Hmm, so there are some fancy words in the lyrics. So what?

Student: Well a bunch of big words doesn't make something smarter. You still have to be able to connect to it and understand the message.

The student's explanation makes visible the underlying assumptions that have guided the student's evaluation of the argument. You can see how the scale helped drive the discussion forward, attending to each element of Toulmin's model of argument along the way. Once students have made their reasoning explicit in this manner, we can now push them further. We can ask them to describe some alternatives that would make them change their marks, or we can press them to elaborate further on their data or warrants. What's important is the central role the scale played in both prompting students to generate their responses and in shaping those responses toward the kind of critical thinking we value in our classrooms.

We like using scales for a number of reasons. First, the student's initial response is streamlined into a simple process of selection. We like to think of this as giving our students an "easy in" to a complex conversation. Second, once our students have made that initial selection, they have a clear and visible model to guide them as they are called upon to support and extend their thinking. Third, scales provide the occasion for the repeated use of the Toulmin questions, increasing the likelihood that those prompts will be internalized and called upon in new situations.

Many of our lessons feature examples of SDS to guide students in their responses to texts and other forms of data. Sometimes, we design our scales to scaffold students' readings of challenging texts. Sometimes, we design them to cue students toward important details in the data. As teachers, it can be very helpful to think about these different uses for scales to prepare ourselves for the various ways students may respond to them. Let's briefly go over a few examples to illustrate these different uses.

In one activity, we ask students to read an excerpt from a well-known book, *The Bell Curve* (Herrnstein & Murray, 1994). The excerpt is taken from the chapter titled "Ethnic Differences in Cognitive Ability," and it begins with the following passage:

> Despite the forbidding air that envelops the topic, ethnic differences in cognitive ability are neither surprising nor in doubt. Large human populations differ in many ways, both cultural and biological. It is not surprising that they might differ at least slightly in their cognitive characteristics. That they do is confirmed by the data on ethnic differences in cognitive ability from around the world. One message of this chapter is that such differences are real and have consequences. Another is that the facts are not as alarming as many people seem to fear. (p. 269)

After reading this passage, students are asked to respond to the following scale.

The authors will argue that the basis of intelligence is:

This scale, designed to scaffold students' reading of a challenging text, allows for a range of possible responses. However, given the argument set forth in the text, there are a few places on this scale that would be difficult, if not impossible, to support. A student who marks Position 6 or 7 (or perhaps even Position 5) is probably struggling to comprehend the argument here. In this respect, the scale gives us both valuable feedback into that student's reading, as well as a visible tool with which we can help that student to see where he or she may be missing something important in the passage.

In the previous example, the SDS is designed in such a way that every position on the scale cannot be reasonably supported. Sometimes SDSs are designed to elicit a somewhat different kind of response. For example, the scenario above, where the student is asked to respond to an author's entire argument by marking the convincing–unconvincing scale, offers the full range of potential marks on the scale. What matters in this case is both how the student is able to support and justify the mark, and how mindful the student is about the strength or magnitude of his or her commitment to the mark. A student who marks Position 1, for example, adopts a fully committed stance. As that student sees it, the author's argument is absolutely flawless and beyond dispute. On the other hand, a student who marks Position 4 is taking a middle ground. That student must account for both strengths of the argument as well as ways in which it could be challenged. In this respect, the scale gives us an opportunity to press the student's reasoning and prompt the student to consider possible weaknesses or potential counterarguments.

CONSIDER THIS

Think of a favorite text you have used with students on a number of different occasions. Has teaching the text ever caused you to understand or respond to it differently based on how your students have responded? How might SDSs help students to understand their own changing relationships with the texts they read?

Much like Osgood and his colleagues, we appreciate the ways that SDSs help us and our students get a glimpse into the processes by which they are making meaning. SDSs provide a helpful model for students as they respond to texts and other forms and data, and they also give us valuable insights into their thinking so that we can provide them with clear and useful feedback (Imbrenda, 2016). SDSs are a flexible tool. Students can write out their responses, share them out loud in full-class discussions, or share them in small groups or pairs. We most often use 7-point scales, but we might use a 6-point scale in order to force students to be at least somewhat positioned as there is no middle ground. Or we might use a 5-point scale to restrict the range of options and make it easier to jump in. We adapt them to meet our needs, our students' preferences, and the circumstances of our classrooms on any given day.

Paragraph Frames

The final tool we employ is the paragraph frame. We use these frames to help students put the talking they have been doing into effective written expression. Because the frames are an essential part of our practice, we think they merit a little bit of explanation.

Jon-Philip began his career teaching freshman composition at a small college. In his department, there were often debates about how to best teach incoming students how to write academic arguments. The debates centered on a single idea: Should we be teaching language or should we be teaching content? Those who embraced the former position argued that in order to become a writer of academic arguments, instruction needed to focus on the formal and stylistic features of academic texts. Those who embraced the latter position argued that in order to become a writer of academic arguments, instruction needed to focus on exploring bold ideas, generating discussion around those ideas, and then sending the students off to communicate their ideas in writing. These debates happened over a decade ago, and since that time Jon-Philip, guided by the work of many literacy scholars, has come to understand that the two sides of the debate are actually expressions of two different dimensions of a single, integrated process. Understanding the formal features of academic arguments and understanding the things you need to fit into those formal features are the same thing.

Graff and Birkenstein (2010), in their immensely popular book *They Say/I Say: The Moves That Matter in Academic Writing*, demonstrate a similar understanding. They introduce a vast array of sentence templates designed to focus students' attentions on both what they're saying as well as how they're saying it. The templates represent many of the linguistic constructions common to academic argumentation. Furthermore, they reflect an explicit appreciation for the ways in which academic writing enters into ongoing conversations within culturally relevant domains.

As you've already seen, we share Graff and Birkenstein's (2010) appreciation for the conversation metaphor, and we admire the ingenuity of the templates they present. Although they have been an important influence on our instructional thinking, we also take things a step further by expanding their single or dual sentence frames into complete paragraphs, making the linguistic cues we provide students with more consistent with Toulmin's model of argument, and designing templates that are specific to the texts or data students are working with. We call these expanded templates *paragraph frames*.

Our paragraph frames have a dual function. They give students clear scaffolding to help them communicate their ideas in the unique language of academic writing. At the same time, they also apprentice students into the ways of reasoning that are most valued in academic communities of practice. For some of us, that language and the underlying ways of reasoning it conveys may not seem so strange. But for many of our students, including the ones we've been working with these past few years, the language and modes of reasoning that characterize academic discourse seem quite strange and impractical. Our paragraph frames are designed to help them gradually acculturate into the linguistic conventions as well as the habits of thinking those conventions are meant to maintain. As we said above, we believe the two are inextricably related. That's why we like using the frames! They give students a good amount of structure to guide their writing without doing any of the heavy lifting for them.

Our frames typically map on closely to the elements of argument we described in the previous chapter. In completing a frame, students are prompted to generate one or more claims, supply data to support those claims, and give explicit warrants to connect the data to the claims. We also design them with a concern for certain strategies—such as clearly identifying sources or providing succinct and accurate summaries—that we know are important hallmarks of successful academic writing. Throughout the school year, as students consistently complete frames, they gradually internalize the linguistic structures and find themselves calling upon them on their own when they are asked to compose extended arguments with less explicit guidance.

Here's a frame we use early in our "What Does It Really Mean to Be Smart?" unit. We introduce it after students have read a short article by a clinical psychologist staking out the position that intelligence is a function of how resourceful a person is, how well a person can interact with others, and how well a person can solve practical problems:

> Dr. Ben Michaelis offers a view of intelligence that is [*similar to/ different from*] what many people expect. The central argument of his view is [*state the author's main CLAIM in your own words*]. He supports this position by [*briefly describe the DATA from which his claim is drawn*]. The general belief behind his position can be summed up as [*in your own words, explain how the author WARRANTS his position*]. I [*agree/disagree*] with Dr. Michaelis [*completely/to a certain extent*] because [*summarize why you agree or disagree.*]

We see these short writings as developmental practice for them and as formative assessment for us.

Because it's early in the unit, we're focusing on having students analyze someone else's argument as a way to scaffold the production of their own, something they'll do increasingly as the unit progresses. We're also providing practice in summarizing and forcing students to attend to the text. Finally, the frame makes clear that the argument is genuine. Whereas students' summaries should resemble each other, their responses to those summaries will vary, requiring them to produce fully formed arguments in order to be persuasive.

You'll see other examples of paragraph frames throughout this book, each of which was part of students' ongoing "writing portfolios." We use this designation to make it clear that we see these short writings as developmental practice for them and as formative assessment for us. We don't introduce the writing portfolios right away, nor do we use them all the time. Most of our lessons have some kind of writing portfolio activity, though, and many of those activities are strategically designed paragraph frames.

Once again, our tools are consistent with our metaphor of conversation. Paragraph frames help students become legitimate participants in the kinds of conversations that take place in academic communities of practice. In this case, they are focused on the written conversations that are central to the ways that participants in academic communities generate and share knowledge, critique one another's understandings, and contribute to the breadth and depth of their respective disciplines.

So Do They Work?

One of the things that we've come to realize in our work at the urban comprehensive school at which we taught the lessons we're sharing here is that teachers face a paradoxical challenge. It is our job to prepare students for tomorrow, but we can only do so by engaging them today in issues that matter in the here and now (cf. Smith & Wilhelm, 2002). Many of the students with whom we work see the academy and academic argumentation as something foreign and distant. We try to bridge the gaps by introducing argumentative reasoning and the writing of arguments through activities that are close to home. For instance, our students were thinking about their college options when we taught Lesson 19, which asks them to apply argumentative reasoning as they consider the benefits and consequences of choosing 2-year or 4-year colleges, so we were teaching for tomorrow with materials that matter today. The 20 lessons in the coming chapters are designed to apprentice students into the kind of academic conversations in which we want them to be able to participate. Each of our lessons has a brief introduction, a step-by-step plan, a dataset of some sort or another, a tool we used, and an example of students' work and our commentary on that example.

We've tried all of these lessons in the Pathways project to great effect. We have 2 years of data now and have achieved a statistically significant growth both years for both the eleventh and twelfth graders with whom we worked. We're especially pleased with the magnitude of the change. The magnitude of the impact of an intervention is assessed with a statistic known as the partial eta squared. We won't bore you with the details except to say that the threshold for large effects is 0.138 (Cohen, 1992). In both years of our project, our effect size was over twice that threshold (0.381 in Year 1 and 0.395 in Year 2). In short, the lessons we will be sharing worked for us. We think they will work for you as well.

It is our job to prepare students for tomorrow, but we can only do so by engaging them today in issues that matter in the here and now.

PART II

Lessons

Chapter 4

Everyday Arguments

Introducing the Elements of Argument

As we've explained in Chapter 2, we base our instruction in argument on Stephen Toulmin's (1958) model. Toulmin appeals to us because he focuses on everyday argumentation, so we think his work provides a great way to link what students already do outside of class to what we want them to do in class. The purpose of the lessons in this chapter is to engage students in conversations that require them to produce the three essential elements of any argument:

1. *Claim* (what you're arguing for)

2. *Data* (the evidence you use)

3. *Warrant* (an explanation of the principles that link the data to the claim)

Apple Music vs. Spotify

LESSON PLAN

Purpose/Learning Intentions: Engage in everyday arguments to learn the relationship between *data* and *warrant*. Use data to make an everyday argument, explain the significance of data by articulating a warrant, and practice evaluating the importance of details.

Length: Approximately 45 minutes (two class periods or one block)

Materials Needed

- A class set of Handout 1.1, "Apple Music vs. Spotify"

- A class set of Handout 1.2, "Planning Your Argument"

- Whiteboard, chart paper, or other means of recording students' responses

Lesson Steps

Step 1: Introduce students to the idea of everyday argument.

- Explain to students that much of their success in school, especially as they go on to college, will depend on their ability to write effective arguments.

- Explain that the good news is that they are all expert arguers already.

- Explain that whether we're deciding which new smartphone to upgrade to, or deciding what outfit to wear to school that day, we're engaging in a process of argumentative reasoning.

- Give a personal illustration. For example, explain that when you're choosing a restaurant, you have to determine the cost, quality, and location before making a choice.

UNIT CONTEXT:

Arguments in our everyday lives. We suggest using this as the first lesson in the everyday argument section.

LESSON BACKGROUND:

By comparing two similar music streaming services, students must attend to details in the *data* to highlight what they view as key differences. Their *warrants*, therefore, will reflect the reasons why they see certain details as being more important than others. Making comparisons then becomes not just a matter of noticing details in the *data*, but also of evaluating the *importance* of those details with respect to the student's personal values and assumptions. By examining their warrants, students will begin to understand that arguments often represent a kind of reasoning in which personal values and interests influence the choices we make.

Step 2: Engage students in planning for an argument about which music streaming service is a better choice: Apple Music or Spotify.

- Distribute Handout 1.1.

- Emphasize that you will expect students to build their argument using the data you provide. If students ask what you mean about data, explain that it's just another word for evidence.

- To guide students in examining the data, instruct them to work individually to do as follows:

  → First, lightly cross off details that will be irrelevant to their argument. They should start by crossing off similarities. For example, both Apple Music and Spotify allow users to share playlists so that detail from the data will not be relevant to their argument.

  → Then, tell them cross off additional details that are different across both options but unimportant.

  → Finally, have them circle three to five key details in the data that they feel are essential to their decision.

Step 3: Have a whole-class discussion about their choices.

- Get a sense of the whole class by asking students to indicate which streaming service they chose by raising their hands.

- Choose one student and ask him or her to explain why.

- Be consistent in the prompts you use to generate the elements of the model:

  → Where do you stand? (claim)

  → What makes you say so? (data)

  → So what? (warrant)

- Ask a student who took a different position to explain why. Once again be consistent in the prompts you use to generate the elements of the model:

  → Where do you stand? (claim)

  → What makes you say so? (data)

  → So what? (warrant)

- Continue discussion until the arguments start to get repetitious.

Step 4: Have students transfer their oral work into writing.

- Distribute Handout 1.2.

- Instruct students to work individually to plan their brief arguments by using Handout 1.2.

- As they work, circulate. If students have difficulty, prompt them by referring back to the whole-class discussion.

- Once they have finished their planning on the graphic organizer, have them write a brief paragraph. Once again, make sure to circulate as they are doing their work.

Step 5: Have students share their work in pairs.

- Ask them to circle their partner's claim, that is, the answer to the "Where do you stand?" question, on their partner's work.

- Ask them to put in brackets each piece of data, that is, the answer to the "What makes you say so?" question.

- Ask them to underline each warrant, that is, the answer to the "So what?" question.

- Have partners discuss what elements of their arguments work best and which ones might need improvement.

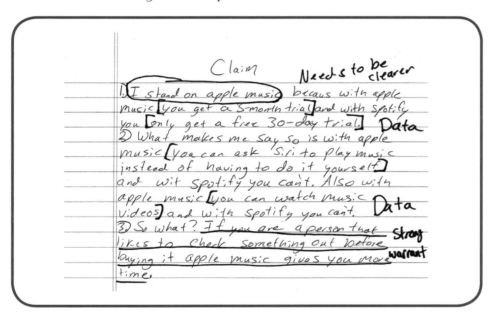

Step 6: Summarize key points from the class.

- Remind students that they make arguments all the time in their everyday life.

- Explain that these arguments require them both to think about data and to think about why those data matter, what we call a warrant.

Extension: Have students consider what data that's *not* on the table might be important and to fill out Handout 1.2 to develop an argument from those data.

Apple Music vs. Spotify

	APPLE MUSIC	SPOTIFY
What devices can use it?	Mac computers with OS 10.9.5 or newer; PC with Windows 7 or newer. Computers must have iTunes 12.2 iPhone 4 or newer iPad 2 or newer iPod Touch 5 or newer	Web-based streaming is compatible with any PC or Mac computer. Spotify App is compatible with any Android or iPhone as well as Windows 8 phones, iPad, PlayStation 4, and XBOX One. Retailers offer a wide range of Spotify-ready devices such as portable music players and home stereo systems.
How can you try it out?	3-month trial streaming with ads	30-day trial shuffle streaming with ads
What does it cost?	$10/month for a single subscription $15/month for a family plan of up to 6 people	$10/month for a single subscription $5/month per additional person $5/month for students
How much music does it offer?	Unconfirmed as of now, but Apple has promised that the song library will be comparable to Spotify.	Over 30 million tracks
Can I play music offline?	Yes, with subscription	Yes, with subscription
What social features are included?	Share playlists.	Share playlists. Collaborate on playlists. See what friends are listening to.
What other features are included?	iPhone users can search for music using Siri voice commands. Watch music videos. Apple currently has an exclusive contract with Taylor Swift to stream her new album; similar contracts with other artists are promised for the future.	Listen to podcasts. Read song lyrics.

online resources 🔎 Available for download at **resources.corwin.com/writersofargument**

Planning Your Argument

Make your *claim*!

This is pretty easy here! Just tell us which music service you've chosen.

```
┌────────────────────────────────────────────────────────────┐
│                                                              │
│                                                              │
│                                                              │
│                                                              │
└────────────────────────────────────────────────────────────┘
```

Based on

```
┌────────────────────────────────────────────────────────────┐
│   1.                                                         │
│                                                              │
│   2.                                                         │
│                                                              │
│   3.                                                         │
│                                                              │
└────────────────────────────────────────────────────────────┘
```

Show your *data*! List the key differences between the two options that have led to your claim.

Which is important because . . .

```
┌────────────────────────────────────────────────────────────┐
│                                                              │
│                                                              │
│                                                              │
│                                                              │
└────────────────────────────────────────────────────────────┘
```

Now, you have to *warrant* your choice by explaining why the differences you noticed in the data are important to you. Think about each difference individually, but look for patterns in your reasoning. Is there a general "rule" that you could apply?

Now that you've done all that planning, put it all together in a short paragraph.

```
┌────────────────────────────────────────────────────────────┐
│                                                              │
│                                                              │
│                                                              │
│                                                              │
│                                                              │
│                                                              │
│                                                              │
└────────────────────────────────────────────────────────────┘
```

JENNIFER
Grade 11

Jennifer makes a clear claim here, but she embeds a piece of data in it.

She's developing the idea that she needs to support her claims with data, but her writing is list-like with no explicit warrants. Maybe she had trouble translating the graphic organizer.

She understands data and hints at warrants. She needs more practice and instruction on articulating the general principles that link her data and her claim.

I would rather use Spotify than Apple Music because it would be cheaper for me because I'm a student. I prefer it because I can also listen to podcasts as well as music. I can learn the songs faster and sing along while reading the lyrics on Spotify, while I can't using Apple Music. I prefer Spotify because it is confirmed that they have a larger amount of music and I prefer to listen to Alternative music, making it a greater chance to hear the songs I know.

Moving Forward

- Everyday arguments are working well for Jennifer, as she demonstrates a clear understanding of claims and data, and begins to allude to warrants.

- We can support Jennifer's progress by emphasizing the importance of explicit warrants as a way to strengthen her argument by making her reasoning more visible.

Taco Bell vs. Chipotle

LESSON PLAN

Purpose/Learning Intentions: Engage in an everyday argument to begin to internalize the Toulmin question prompts.

Length: Approximately 45 minutes

Materials Needed

- A class set of Handout 2.1, "Taco Bell vs. Chipotle"

- Whiteboard, chart paper, or other means of recording students' responses

Lesson Steps

Step 1: Relate this lesson to yesterday's.

- Remind students that yesterday we had our first lesson on everyday argument.

- Ask students to name the three elements of argument that we learned. When a student responds, with claim, data, or warrant, ask, "What question does claim/data/warrant answer?"

- Record the elements and the questions that elicit them on the board or on an anchor chart:

  → Claim: Where do you stand?

  → Data: What makes you say so?

  → Warrant: So what?

- Explain to students that we're going to keep asking the same questions the same way so that they will become second nature to them.

- Explain that this time, though, we're moving from music, one of their favorite things, to food, another favorite.

UNIT CONTEXT:

Arguments in our everyday lives. We suggest using this as the second lesson in the everyday argument section.

LESSON BACKGROUND:

As we've explained, we find the Toulmin model especially useful because it maps on so well to the way arguments work in everyday conversation. That's important, because, as we noted in Chapter 2, children as young as 3 can produce all of the elements of an effective argument with the prompting of a conversational partner (Stein & Albro, 2001). Of course, students won't have a conversational partner when they write, so we want them to internalize the conversational prompts we use so they can employ them when they write.

Step 2: Engage students in planning for an argument about who makes the better burrito: Taco Bell or Chipotle.

- Distribute Handout 2.1.

- Ask students to read the handout carefully and to decide which burrito they will choose. Encourage them to use highlighters to identify data they find especially compelling and to think about the warrant for each piece of data.

Step 3: Divide students into pairs to rehearse their argument. To the extent possible, pair students who made different choices.

- Explain to students that you want them to play the role you did yesterday and to prompt their partner's argument by using the Toulmin questions.

- Explain that almost every argument has more than one piece of data so that students should ask, "What else makes you say so?" until the partner no longer has data that support his or her claim.

- Circulate as students are working. Listen to make sure that they are using the Toulmin probes. Try to attend to the range of evidence students are posing. Remind them that warrants are general rules. If anyone is having difficulty, point to where they are recorded on the board and encourage them to use the board as a resource.

Step 4: Convene the whole class for a discussion.

- Ask, "Who chose Taco Bell?" Get a show of hands. Pick one student and ask him or her to explain why.

- As always be consistent in the prompts you use to generate the elements of the model:

    → Where do you stand? (claim)

    → What makes you say so? (data)

    → So what? (warrant)

- Ask a student who took the other position to explain why. Once again, be consistent in the prompts you use to generate the elements of the model:

    → Where do you stand? (claim)

    → What makes you say so? (data)

    → So what? (warrant)

- Continue the discussion, alternating between advocates of Taco Bell and Chipotle until the arguments start to get repetitive.

Step 5: Have students put their arguments into writing.

- Remind them to make sure they answer all of the questions.

- Encourage them to draw on the details of Handout 2.1 as they do their work.

Step 6: Have students share their work in pairs.

- Have students return to their original pairings.

- Have them repeat the process they used in yesterday's lesson:

  → Ask them to circle their partner's claim, that is, the answer to the "Where do you stand?" question.

  → Ask them to put in brackets each piece of data, that is, the answer to the "What makes you say so?" question.

  → Ask them to underline each warrant, that is, the answer to the "So what?" question.

- Have partners discuss what elements of their arguments work best and which ones might need improvement.

Step 7: Summarize key points from the class.

- Remind students that the Toulmin questions will be useful.

- Explain that these arguments require them both to think about data and to think about why those data matter, what we call a warrant.

Extension: Have students develop a t-chart for another menu item comparison and write another paragraph in which they use the Toulmin probes to craft their argument.

Taco Bell vs. Chipotle

	TACO BELL	CHIPOTLE
Average Cost	$2.29	$6.25
Nutritional Content	Calories: 390; Calories from fat: 100; Total fat: 12g; Trans-fat: 0g; Sodium: 1090mg; Cholesterol: 40mg; Carbohydrates: 50g; Dietary fiber: 6g; Sugar: 4g; Protein: 20g; Vitamin C: 8%; Vitamin A: 10%; Calcium: 20%; Iron: 20%	Calories: 735; Calories from fat: 226; Total fat: 26g; Trans-fat: 0g; Sodium: 1990mg; Cholesterol: 155mg; Carbohydrates: 74g; Dietary fiber: 16g; Sugar: 2g; Protein: 52g; Vitamin C: 42%; Vitamin A: 110%; Calcium: 50%; Iron: 40%
Options	Mild, Hot, or Fire Sauce; Salsa Verde	White or brown rice; black or pinto beans; mild, medium, hot, or corn salsa; vegetables; add guacamole for approximately $2
Quality of Ingredients	Low-grade, industrial-farmed meats and cheeses	Locally sourced meats, cheeses, and vegetables from humane-certified farms
Locations and Hours of Operation	6,500 locations; open 11 AM–1 AM; eat-in, carry out, drive through	2,010 locations; open 11 AM–10 PM; eat-in or carry out

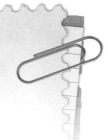

ANDREW
Grade 11

I would choose Chipotle out of the two options. I am a fitness freak. I love everything that's high on protein. As provided in the given data, Chipotle is low on sugars, cholesterol, and trans-fat. Chipotle's burrito provides 2 sets of vitamins, calcium, and iron. Also, Chipotle offers a couple types of rice and beans, 4 types of salsa, and veggies. If you are someone that cares for fitness such as me, you'll prefer this burrito. It's high on protein, vitamins, calcium, iron, and dietary fiber.

Andrew presents a clear claim up front. However, he should be explicit about both of the things he is comparing.

He evidences concern for his reader by framing his claim in the context of his personal values.

These are excellent and specific data. Some specific references to the object of his comparison (Taco Bell) would help, though.

Andrew does a great job of separating his warrant out into a statement of a general principle.

Moving Forward

- By providing a clear summary of his data, Andrew demonstrates mindfulness of an audience beyond the classroom. We need to make sure his classmates do so as well.

- We need to make sure that students understand they need to present both sides when making a comparative argument.

Who Is the Better Superhero?

Arguments in our everyday lives

LESSON BACKGROUND:

One of the things we want students to recognize is that the elements of argument with which they are working are intimately related. One of the purposes of this lesson is to help students understand how an a priori understanding of potential warrants will help them generate data and clarify their claims.

LESSON PLAN

Purpose/Learning Intentions: Understand how potential warrants will help you as both a reader and a writer.

Length: Approximately 45 minutes

Materials Needed

- A class set of Handout 3.1, "What Makes a Good Superhero?"

- A class set of Handout 3.2, "Batman vs. Superman"

- A class set of Handout 3.3, "Planning Your Argument"

- Whiteboard, chart paper, or other means of recording students' responses

Lesson Steps

Step 1: Relate this lesson to yesterday's.

- Remind students that yesterday we continued our work with everyday arguments and that they have had practice working with all three elements: data, warrants, and claims.

- Ask students to respond in choral fashion to the question associated with each element:

  Teacher: What question does a claim answer?

  Student: *Where do you stand?*

  Teacher: What question do data answer?

  Student: *What makes you say so?*

  Teacher: What question does a warrant answer?

  Student: *So what?*

- Explain that today we're going to turn our attention from music and food to comic books and TV and consider the question "What makes a good superhero?"

Step 2: Generate criteria for what makes a good superhero.

- Distribute Handout 3.1. Ask students to rank the items on the handout. As they do so, circulate to see what new characteristics students are adding.

- Begin a whole-class discussion by soliciting new characteristics. List those on the board.

- Give students a few minutes to factor the new characteristics into their ranking.

- Begin a whole-class discussion by asking a student, "What did you rank as number 1?" Use Toulmin questions to probe for his or her reasoning:

  → What makes you say so?

  → So what?

- Ask, "How many of you agree?" Turn to a student who disagreed and follow the same procedure for the characteristic he or she selected as #1. Once again, use Toulmin questions to probe for his or her reasoning.

- Continue the process until the discussion loses energy or students have had a chance to share their top three characteristics.

Step 3: Draw on discussion to inform their reading.

- Explain that today they'll be considering who makes the better superhero, Batman or Superman. Note that the discussion they just had should provide the basis for their argument and that in fact, what they were just debating is what warrants they should use in making their case.

- Distribute Handout 3.2. Explain that they should read the handout being mindful of the argument that they will be making. Explain that one way to think about what they are doing is "mining" the text to select what's most valuable so they can then use what they mined to talk and write. Encourage them to use highlighters to identify what they mined.

- Give students an opportunity to read the handout.

Step 4: Divide students into pairs to rehearse their argument. To the extent possible, pair students who made different choices.

- Ask students to write down which superhero they will be advocating for.

- Have all of the students who chose Batman to stand up. Explain that you want each Batman advocate to find a Superman advocate and to debate the issue in pairs. If the numbers are not divided equally, allow some debates to be in groups of three.

- As pairs are debating, circulate to listen to their arguments. If some debates are losing energy before the majority of the class, use the Toulmin questions to help students with their discussions.

Step 5: Have students write out their arguments.

- Distribute Handout 3.3. Note that this handout is a bit different from their previous planning sheet in that it shows how having a sense of the warrant helps determine what are the best data.

- Have students work on their planning sheet and once they have done so to write a paragraph arguing for their selection.

Step 6: Have students share their work in pairs.

- Have students return to their original pairings.

- Have them switch papers and repeat the process they used in the previous two lessons:

  → Circle the claim; that is, circle the answer to the "Where do you stand?" question, on their partner's work.

- Ask them to put in brackets each piece of data; that is, bracket the answer to the "What makes you say so?" question.

- Ask them to underline each warrant; that is, underline the answer to the "So what?" question.

- Have partners discuss what elements of their arguments work best and which ones might need improvement.

Extension: Have students imagine that they are going to buy a new car to drive when they are in college. Have them list what they think are the five most important criteria they would use in making that purchase. Using those warrants, have them mine a website to determine what choice they would make.

What Makes a Good Superhero?

Rank these characteristics from the one that is most important to being a good superhero (1) to the one that is least important to being a good hero (8). If you want to add a characteristic that's not included, please do and include it in your rankings.

_____ A good name

_____ A good costume

_____ A good power

_____ An interesting history

_____ Being easy to relate to

_____ Being a good role model

_____ Being funny

_____ Having good villains to oppose

_____ Other (please specify)

 Available for download at **resources.corwin.com/writersofargument**

Batman vs. Superman

	BATMAN	SUPERMAN
Species	Human	Kryptonian
Abilities	Peak human capacity in intelligence, physical conditioning, and willpower. Master of martial arts. Expert in military tactics, forensic science, and espionage. Designer of high-tech gadgets, vehicles, and armor.	Peak superhuman levels of strength, speed, stamina, and endurance. Invulnerable to physical harm. Can fly at supersonic speeds. Thermal vision. Super breath. Enhanced senses.
Alter Ego	Bruce Wayne, billionaire CEO of Wayne Industries	Clark Kent, mild-mannered reporter for *The Daily Planet*
Weaknesses	Relies on gadgets and armor	Vulnerable to green kryptonite
Symbolism	Strikes fear and terror in the hearts of criminals	Serves truth, justice, and the American way
Heroic Origin	After witnessing the murder of his parents at the hands of a desperate criminal, young Bruce Wayne devoted himself to a vigilante lifestyle. He tapped into his family's tremendous resources to develop crime-fighting technology, while undergoing intensive physical and mental training.	After the destruction of his home planet, Krypton, Superman, an infant at the time, was sent to Earth by his parents. Adopted by humble farmers and raised as a typical American boy, young Clark began to discover his extraordinary powers during his adolescence. Eventually, his adopted father revealed his true origin to him.

Planning Your Argument

A good superhero has to have these qualities:

1.

2.

3.

Therefore:

Make your *claim*!

Which hero has those qualities?

Show your *data*! Explain how you know that your hero has those qualities and the other hero doesn't.

1.

2.

3.

4.

5.

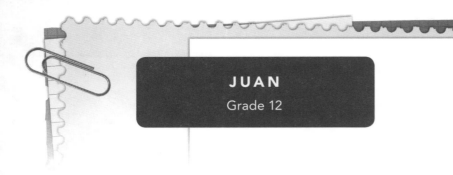

Juan makes an interesting move here by embedding his warrant in his claim.

He might want to reorganize these data points a bit. He seems to be undecided as to whether he wants to compare by character or by attribute.

Juan does a great job of referring back to warrant, but his moves would be more effective if he more clearly articulated his reasoning.

I think Batman is a better superhero because his civilian life and background are more interesting and realistic. What makes me say that is superman is an alien and Batman was born on Earth and even though he is rich he's still human. So there Batman is vulnerable. He can die, making his dedication more meaningful. Superman, on the other hand, is invincible so he can walk through bombs making his motives less realistic.

Moving Forward

- We've helped Juan to develop a complete argument with all of the necessary elements.

- Juan seems to understand all of the elements of argument, but we need to work with him to elaborate his ideas for his audience.

- Juan will probably benefit from the use of paragraph templates to help him organize his arguments into common rhetorical structures.

Which Video Streaming Service Is the Best?

LESSON PLAN

Purpose/Learning Intentions: Understand and demonstrate your ability to put your arguments into academic language.

Length: Approximately 45 minutes

Materials Needed

- A class set of Handout 4.1, "Netflix vs. Hulu Plus vs. Amazon Prime"

- A class set of Handout 4.2, "Paragraph Frame for Streaming Services" (Or if all of your students have devices, an electronic version of the frame on Google Docs)

- Whiteboard, chart paper, or other means of recording students' responses

Lesson Steps

Step 1: Relate lesson to previous lessons.

- Remind students that you've been working with everyday arguments because they are expert at them, but that you've been working to look at those arguments so that students can see how they are structured.

- Ask what element of argument answers the question "Where do you stand?" How about "What makes you say so?" And what answers the question "So what?"

Step 2: Introduce the argument about streaming services.

- Explain that today they'll be considering which streaming service they would choose: Netflix, Hulu Plus, or Amazon Prime.

UNIT CONTEXT:

Arguments in our everyday lives

LESSON BACKGROUND:

In our fourth introductory lesson, we ratchet up the rigor in two ways. First, we ask students to compare three items instead of just two. Second, we introduce the idea that claims may not be absolute, that is, that students may have to qualify their claims in some way depending on the audience for which they are writing. We also introduce one of the tools that we will be using throughout, the paragraph frame. The frame is designed to provide a scaffold for students to enable them to put their argument in using the kinds of academic language and syntax that are rewarded in college.

- Recall that yesterday they learned that it's helpful to think about the argument they'll be making before they start reading. Remind them of the work they did "mining" their reading after the discussion of the most important qualities of a superhero.

- Have students do a 2-minute discussion with a partner about the most important features of a streaming service.

Step 3: Read the handout to prepare for the argument.

- Distribute Handout 4.1. Encourage them to use highlighters to identify what they mined.

- Give students an opportunity to read the handout.

Step 4: Have a whole-class discussion.

- Have students write down the service from the one they favor most to the one they favor least.

- Get a sense of the whole by putting a matrix like this one on the board:

	1	2	3
Netflix			
Hulu Plus			
Amazon Prime			

- Ask, "How many of you ranked Netflix as the best service? Second best? Worst?" Mark the tallies in the columns. Repeat the process with the other services.

- Ask for a volunteer to support Netflix. Use the Toulmin questions to encourage students to elaborate.

- Ask for a volunteer to support Hulu Plus. This time in addition to the Toulmin questions, ask the student to factor in what the proponent of Netflix said with questions like "But what about the point that [student's name] made about _____?"

- Continue the whole-class discussion until the energy dissipates.

Step 5: Introduce the paragraph frame.

- Explain that as usual, students will be writing up their arguments, but that this time, you want to help them frame it in a language and a structure like what they'll be expected to use in college.

- Distribute (or display) the paragraph frame (Handout 4.2). Have students work individually to complete the frame. Make sure they write out the whole frame rather than just filling in the blanks as that will make it more likely that they will make it part of their repertoires.

- Ask several volunteers to read their paragraphs.

- Congratulate students on a job well done and encourage them to use what they learned from the frame in their future writing.

Extension: Have students use Handout 4.3, "Paragraph Frame for Product of Students' Own Choosing," to compare three products/services of their own choosing.

Netflix vs. Hulu Plus vs. Amazon Prime

	NETFLIX	HULU PLUS	AMAZON PRIME
Cost of service	$8.99 per month for unlimited streaming	$7.99 per month for unlimited streaming	$99 per year or $49 per year for students
What can you watch?	Movies, television shows, and original series. Licensing deals with CBS, ABC, Fox, Starz, NBC, BBC, Sony, and DreamWorks. Catalog is updated monthly. Total selection is approximately 25,000 titles.	Movies, television shows, and original series. Licensing deals with Fox, Disney, NBC, MTV, TBS, Cartoon Network, TNT, Adult Swim, and FX. Catalog is updated weekly. Total selection is approximately 15,000 titles.	Movies, television shows, and original series. Licensing deals with CBS and other networks for exclusive rights to specific shows. Also has exclusive rights to HBO shows. Catalog is updated monthly. Total selection is approximately 10,000 titles.
What can you watch it on?	Smart TVs, Roku, XBOX, PlayStation, Nintendo, Apple or Android phones and tablets, PC or Mac computers	Smart TVs, Roku, XBOX, PlayStation, Nintendo, Apple or Android phones and tablets, PC or Mac computers	Smart TVs, Roku, XBOX, PlayStation, Nintendo, Apple or Android phones and tablets, PC or Mac computers
What else do you get?	Commercial-free streaming. Can rate titles and receive recommendations. Share viewing activity with friends.	Has commercials, but allows for the fastest access to new episodes of television shows.	Also includes subscription to Amazon's music streaming service; free shipping on retail purchases.
Popular original series	*Orange Is the New Black* *House of Cards* *Daredevil*	*Behind the Mask* *Blue* *Difficult People*	*Transparent* *Red Oaks* *Catastrophe*

 Available for download at **resources.corwin.com/writersofargument**

Paragraph Frame for Streaming Services

Among the three options for video streaming services, [*your claim*] is the best choice. Unlike [*one of the options you didn't choose*], which offers [*data point*] and [*data point*], [*your claim*] is a better option because it offers [*data point*] and [*data point*]. When it comes to choosing a video streaming service, the most important thing to consider is [*warrant*]. However, if [*give a condition in which your warrant wouldn't apply*], [*choose another service*] might actually be a better choice because [*give data to support an alternative choice*].

Paragraph Frame for Product
of Students' Own Choosing

Among the three options for _____, [*your claim*] is the best choice. Unlike [*one of the options you didn't choose*], which offers [*data point*] and [*data point*], [*your claim*] is a better option because it offers [*data point*] and [*data point*]. When it comes to choosing _____, the most important thing to consider is [*warrant*]. However, if [*give a condition in which your warrant wouldn't apply*], [*choose another product*] might actually be a better choice because [*give data to support an alternative choice*].

BREANNA
Grade 12

Among the three options for video streaming services, Netflix is the best choice. Unlike Hulu Plus which has a limited selection and fewer TV shows. When it comes to choosing a video streaming service the most important thing to consider is the selection of TV shows and episode count for the shows. However, if you were to base your choice off of newer TV shows, then Hulu Plus might actually be a better choice because Hulu Plus usually plays the episode right after it airs on TV.

> Breanna makes the right move by setting up a contrast, but she struggles with sentence boundaries.

> Her warrant is logical and explicit.

> She shows careful reasoning by anticipating a potential counterargument.

Moving Forward

- We need to help students work closely with the paragraph templates we provide until we're more confident that they have internalized the organizational patterns reflected in the templates.

- Our class discussions should take up the question of "How much data is enough?"

Heinz's Dilemma

Arguments in our everyday lives. This lesson could also be the introductory lesson for a unit on the essential question "To what extent am I responsible to others?"

LESSON BACKGROUND:

The lesson is designed to engage students in the production of warrants. It does so because the facts of the case are clear, so the argument hinges on the production of warrants. It is also designed to get students thinking about hypotheticals, a kind of evidence commonly used in definitions and in philosophical arguments.

You probably recognize Heinz's dilemma from the work of Lawrence Kohlberg. You might notice that we revised Kohlberg's work in two important ways. First, we lowered the price the chemist was asking. Second, we were explicit about the social cost that resulted from Heinz's action. We made these revisions because we thought that without them, the vast majority of our

LESSON PLAN

Purpose/Learning Intentions: Consider the question of one's responsibility to one's family versus one's responsibility to the larger society and know, understand, and demonstrate how to produce warrants as a step in building ethical arguments.

Length: Approximately 90 minutes (two class periods or one block)

Materials Needed

- A class set of Handout 5.1, "Heinz's Dilemma"

- Whiteboard, chart paper, or other means of recording students' responses

Lesson Steps

Step 1: Introduce the lesson and its purpose.

- Remind students that they've been working on producing complete and compelling arguments that include a clear, defensible, and controversial claim, data that provide a safe starting point, a warrant that provides a general rule explaining why the data justify the claim, and a consideration of what people who disagree with the claim might say.

- Explain that in this lesson they will be practicing making their arguments by thinking about a very famous moral dilemma.

Step 2: Engage students in considering Heinz's dilemma.

- Read Heinz's dilemma out loud. Tell students to mark the first semantic differential scale once they have finished reading.

- Draw Scale A on the board.

- Tell students you want to get a sense of the whole. Ask how many marked scale Point 1, and tally the responses above the scale point. Repeat the process for the other scale points.

Step 3: Have a whole-class discussion on students' responses.

- Choose one student who marks the scales near one of the poles. Use Toulmin questions to prompt the student to share his or her reasoning saying something like:

    → Okay, your claim is that Heinz/the chemist is entirely right. What makes you say so?

    → After the student has provided data, say, "So what?"

    → Why does that make Heinz/the chemist entirely right?

- After the student has explained, turn to a student who marked the scale closer to the other pole. Say, "But you disagree." Use the Toulmin questions to elicit that student's reasoning.

- Continue the discussion, always using the Toulmin questions and making sure to draw students who marked the scale closer to the center into the conversation.

Step 4: Reflect on the discussion.

- Explain to students that you want to take a quick look at the arguments they made.

- Diagram one on the board, making it look something like this:

Data $\longrightarrow$	Warrant $\longrightarrow$	Claim
Many other people died because Heinz's actions kept them from having access to the drug.	People should always be concerned with the greatest good.	Heinz was wrong to steal the drug.

- Have students work in pairs to diagram, as you did above, one of the other arguments.

- Combine sets of three pairs to form groups of six and have them share their diagrams.

students would have sided with Heinz. Because we want to build bridges between students' oral abilities and their writing abilities, we wanted to make sure that our materials would foster plenty of talk.

- Circulate as groups are sharing.

(End of Day 1 or 45 minutes)

Step 5: Provide additional practice by changing the details of the dilemma.

- Read Scale B.

- Have students mark the scale.

- Tally responses and lead a whole-class discussion in the same fashion as in Step 3.

- Repeat the process with Scale C.

Step 6: Reflect on the discussion.

- Have students choose one argument they found especially compelling and diagram it as they did in Step 4.

- Have five or six student volunteers come up to the board simultaneously and write their diagram.

- Discuss each. For each, ask these familiar questions to provide a safe starting point:

  → Which argument did you find most compelling?

  → What were the data?

  → What makes you say so? What was the warrant? Remember the warrant answers the "So what?" question by proposing a general rule that explains why the data justify the claim.

Step 7: Have students put their diagrams into a short written argument as indicated on Handout 5.1.

- Circulate as students write to provide coaching.

- When students have completed their writing, have them put it in their portfolios.

Extension: Have students select another dilemma (e.g., the overcrowded lifeboat) and write a brief argument indicating their stance on the dilemma.

Heinz's Dilemma

Heinz's wife was dying from a particular type of cancer. Doctors said a new drug might save her. The drug had been discovered by a local chemist, and Heinz tried desperately to buy some, but the chemist was charging 3 times the money it cost to make the drug, and this was much more than Heinz could afford.

Heinz could only raise half the money, even after help from family and friends. He explained to the chemist that his wife was dying and asked if he could have the drug cheaper or pay the rest of the money later. The chemist refused, saying that he had discovered the drug and was going to make money from it. The husband was desperate to save his wife, so later that night, he broke into the chemist's and stole the drug. As a result of Heinz's actions, the drug was never made available to the public, and many others suffering from that type of cancer could not be saved.

Scale A: Who is right in this situation?

Let's consider some hypothetical situations that might provide counterarguments to your position:

Scale B: What if you knew that Heinz didn't actually love his wife and had been cheating on her?

Scale C: What if you knew that the chemist was poor and needed money just as desperately as Heinz?

Scale D: What if you knew that Heinz's wife actually wanted to die and had begged Heinz to let her go?

Writing Portfolio

Develop a brief argument in which you explain and justify your response to Scale A. Your argument should include a *claim* about which person was more or less right in the situation, *data* from the scenario to support your *claim*, and a *warrant* in which you present a rule or principle to govern the extent of a person's responsibility to others.

 Available for download at **resources.corwin.com/writersofargument**

ROBERT
Grade 11

By providing details from the prompt in his claim, Robert shows mindfulness of an audience beyond the classroom.

Robert is developing an understanding of warrants, but it would help if he articulated his general rule and then applied it to the scenario.

Heinz is right in his actions in breaking into the chemist's and stealing the drugs to save his wife. Heinz's actions are justified because he offered all he has got to the chemist and was even willing to be in debt to pay later so he will pay the chemist regardless. More importantly, a case of life and death is involved with regard to Heinz losing his wife. The chemist for his part was aware of all this and still wanted to just make money rather than the primary goal of drug production which is to save lives.

Moving Forward

- Robert shows mindfulness of an audience beyond the classroom. We need to make sure his classmates do as well.

- We need to work on helping students separate their warrants from their data so they can elaborate each individually and make their relationships clear.

To What Extent Am I Responsible to Others?

LESSON PLAN

Purpose/Learning Intentions: Apply the warrants you developed in your discussion on Heinz's dilemma to two more controversial cases.

Length: Approximately 45 minutes

Materials Needed

- A class set of Handout 6.1, "A Short Biography of Pat Tillman"

- A class set of Handout 6.2, "A Short Biography of Mark Zuckerberg"

- Whiteboard, chart paper, or other means of recording students' response

Lesson Steps

Step 1: Introduce the lesson and its purpose.

- Remind students that in their previous class they took up Heinz's dilemma and thought about our responsibility to others. Note that the scenario they considered was a fictional one, but that today they were going to think about responsibility in terms of two real people, Pat Tillman and Mark Zuckerberg.

- Remind students to keep in mind the warrants that they used yesterday as they might be useful criteria in evaluating Tillman and Zuckerberg.

Step 2: Have students read as writers, mining the text details related to responsibility.

- Distribute Handout 6.1.

- Read the handout aloud and encourage students to highlight any details that will help them consider Tillman's responsibility.

UNIT CONTEXT:

To what extent am I responsible to others?

LESSON BACKGROUND:

As you can see, we have students do at least one bit of formal writing in every lesson. This lesson is the last lesson we suggest doing before we take a step back and examine the details of the elements of argument in greater depth. You'll see that the initial sequence moves students to reading increasingly complex texts and toward increasing independence in their writing.

You'll also notice that this lesson, like the previous, involves the semantic differential scale. As we explained in Chapter 3, semantic differential scales focus students' attention on critical issues and give even the most reticent student an easy way into the classroom discussion.

Step 3: Have a whole-class discussion of whether Tillman was foolish or admirable.

- Ask students to mark the scale.

- To get a sense of the whole class, draw the scale on the board and ask, how many people gave Tillman this scale point? Continue until you have all of the tallies.

- Choose a student who gave Tillman a mark near one of the poles of the scale. Use the Toulmin questions to help the student elaborate his or her reasoning.

- Turn to a student who gave Tillman a mark near one of the other poles. Once again use the Toulmin questions to help the student elaborate his or her reasoning.

- Turn to a student who gave Tillman a mark near the center. As usual, use the Toulmin questions to help the student elaborate his or her reasoning.

- Continue the discussion in this way until the energy in the discussion has waned.

Step 4: Have students read as writers, mining the text details related to responsibility.

- Distribute Handout 6.2.

- Read the handout aloud and encourage students to highlight any details that will help them consider Zuckerberg's responsibility.

Step 5: Have small-group discussions of whether Zuckerberg is disgraceful or commendable.

- Ask students to mark the scale.

- Divide class into homogeneous groups of four or five, grouping more reticent students together in their own groups and talkative students in their own groups. Encourage students to discuss how they marked the scale. By this time, students will know the Toulmin questions and will enjoy acting as the teacher for each other.

- Circulate as groups are working, intervening to enliven the discussions as needed by using the Toulmin questions.

Step 6: Have students put their arguments into writing using the prompt on Handout 6.2.

Step 7: Have students work in pairs to respond to each other's work as they had in previous lessons.

- Ask them to circle the claim, that is, the answer to the "Where do you stand?" question, on their partner's work.

- Ask them to put each piece of data, that is, the answer to the "What makes you say so?" question, in brackets.

- Ask them to underline each warrant, that is, the answer to the "So what?" question.

- Have partners discuss what elements of their arguments work best and which ones might need improvement.

Extension: Have students research a person of their own choosing whose responsibility is debatable and have them write an argument in which they defend or critique that person.

A Short Biography of Pat Tillman

As a student at Arizona State University, 22-year-old Pat Tillman proved himself to be a superb athlete. After leading his team to a Rose Bowl victory, he was named the Pac-10 Defensive Player of the Year. Shortly afterward he was drafted by the Arizona Cardinals where he quickly earned a spot as a starter and set a team record for tackles in 2000. After signing a 3-year, $3.6 million contract, it was clear that he had a bright future ahead.

However, in 2002, in wake of the events that occurred on September 11, 2001, Tillman made a surprising decision to quit the NFL and enlist in the armed forces to join the war in Afghanistan. He is quoted as saying, "Sports embodied many of the qualities I deem meaningful. However, these last few years, and especially after recent events, I've come to appreciate just how shallow and insignificant my role is." He joined the army, trained to become a ranger, and served several tours in Iraq before shipping off to Afghanistan.

On April 22, 2004, Tillman was killed in action. Initial reports held that his death was the result of an enemy ambush. Soon after, though, speculation formed around the circumstances of his death. While much controversy around the incident still remains, there is a great deal of evidence suggesting that he was actually killed by friendly fire. Both official reports and eye-witness accounts indicate that Tillman was mistaken as an enemy when he arrived to help his wounded comrades. Furthermore, military officials are accused of withholding this evidence and attempting to cover up the truth. To this day, his family continues to seek answers.

When Tillman died, he left behind his young wife and his two younger brothers. According to Wikipedia, he repeatedly mentioned in his personal journals during wartime service that he drew strength from and deeply valued his closest friendships, parents, wife, and family.

Scale A: Pat Tillman's decision to quit the NFL and join the army was

A Short Biography of Mark Zuckerberg

Mark Zuckerberg was raised in an affluent household in White Plains, NJ. His parents were both well-educated and successful professionals who were able to afford to send him to exclusive private schools. Furthermore, they nurtured his early interest in computers by hiring a private tutor to work with him. Zuckerberg's talent for computer programming started to show itself during his adolescence when he created a program that would later become the music-streaming service Pandora. Both Apple and Microsoft offered to purchase the program for a substantial amount of money, but Zuckerberg refused, insisting instead to give it away for free.

After turning down several lucrative job offers, Zuckerberg enrolled in college at Harvard University, where he quickly developed a reputation as the most talented programmer on campus. During his sophomore year, he developed a program that allowed college students to select courses based on the courses that other users had selected. It was during this time that he started working on an idea for a social networking site. Working in collaboration with his close friends Dustin Moskovitz and Chris Hughes, they launched the site that would soon become known throughout the world as Facebook in June 2004. Zuckerberg's best friend, Eduardo Saverin, provided the initial startup money and was credited as being the co-founder of Facebook when the site originally launched. In less than a year, Facebook had over 1 million users. Zuckerberg soon became one of the world's youngest billionaires.

However, Facebook's meteoric rise was not without controversy. The first major controversy involved three men who were students at Harvard at the same time as Zuckerberg. In 2006, they filed a lawsuit against Zuckerberg claiming that he had falsely befriended them and then stole the idea for Facebook from them. Zuckerberg denied the claim, arguing that they had two very different ideas for social networking sites, but the court found sufficient cause to believe that Zuckerberg's behavior evidenced his intention to steal the idea. The second major controversy involved Facebook co-founder, Eduardo Saverin. In 2005, just before Facebook gained immense popularity, Zuckerberg devised a way to force Saverin out of the company by diluting his shares in the stock. Legally, the matter was settled out of court with both parties agreeing not to discuss the details. Zuckerberg's friendship with Saverin never recovered, and Saverin eventually left America permanently.

Scale B: Mark Zuckerberg's success should be viewed as

1   2   3   4   5   6   7

Disgraceful   Commendable

Writing Portfolio

Develop a brief argument where you compare Tillman and Zuckerberg with respect to their sense of responsibility to others. Your *claim* should assert your view on which person is a better example of what it means to be responsible. Draw upon details from both people's lives as *data*. Then, your *warrant* should be a general principle about responsibility to others that could apply to many different situations.

 Available for download at **resources.corwin.com/writersofargument**

Nakia embeds sub-claims into her summary of key details from the prompt. In doing so, she confuses summary for data.

These last three sentences succinctly present all three elements of an argument.

Pat Tillman was a respectable man. He had the world at his feet with football fame and leading his team to a Rose Bowl victory. He chose to leave the NFL and enter the army. He put the entire country before himself and his career to go protect others. He made everyone's life his responsibility. Mark Zuckerberg had an intelligence for ideas that he spread with the world. He deserves respect just because of how big his companies became but in the end he came out a little short with all the accusations put on him. I think Pat Tillman was a more responsible person. He had a career going for him and let it go for our country. When it comes to responsibility I feel that putting other people before yourself in such a way not only makes you responsible but also a pretty honorable person.

Moving Forward

- Nakia presents a complete argument with all of the elements in play. Her reasoning is quite strong. We need to help her see how she can elaborate her reasoning.

- We can help Nakia gain a better understanding of the key difference between claims and data: namely, that claims can be controversial, and data cannot.

Notes

_____

_____

_____

_____

_____

_____

_____

_____

_____

_____

_____

_____

_____

_____

Chapter 5

Practicing Three Elements of Argument

In our first six lessons, we engaged students in everyday arguments as a way to introduce them to Toulmin's model. Once we've engaged students in everyday arguments, we do a series of lessons that focus specifically on each of the three primary elements of argument. Why after and not before? Vygotsky (1987) helps us understand this choice. He notes that direct instruction in concepts is impossible; that it is, in his words "pedagogically fruitless" (p. 170). We have taken his words to heart in our teaching, so we always try to create contexts in which we engage students in working with a concept and then have them look back to refine their understanding rather than trying to directly teach them the concepts up front.

LESSON 7

Crafting Controversial Claims

LESSON PLAN

Purpose/Learning Intentions: Understand how a claim should be clear, defensible, and controversial. Practice creating data, evaluating data, and applying criteria.

Length: Approximately 45 minutes

Materials Needed

- A class set of Handout 7.1, "Rating Claims"

- Large paper to record and save students' ideas on an anchor chart

Lesson Steps

Step 1: Relate this lesson to what has preceded.

- Remind students that in their previous lesson, we have been engaging in the kind of everyday arguments that they have as a matter of course in their lives. Recall that yesterday, they had practice working with all three of the primary elements of argument: data, warrants, and claims.

- Explain that today we're going to focus specifically on just one of those elements, claims.

Step 2: Generate criteria for what makes a good claim.

- Distribute Handout 7.1.

- Ask students to work individually to fill out the first scale. Once students have marked the scale, have them do a think-pair-share with a classmate to explain and discuss their rating.

- As students talk, circulate to see what students are saying. If discussions are lagging, say, "How did you rate Mrs. Herzog's claim? What makes you say so?"

UNIT CONTEXT:

Practicing with the elements of argument. This is the first in the series of six lessons.

LESSON BACKGROUND:

When we think back on our work with students over many years, we're a bit embarrassed about the work that we did on claims. Sometimes we preempted the need for students to craft their own claims by providing the claim we wanted them to consider in our writing prompt. But we also ran into problems when we asked students to make their own claims. We realize that we spent far too much time in our careers teaching students how to defend untenable or uninteresting claims instead of teaching them the importance of crafting claims that are both defensible and sufficiently controversial to be of interest. The first two lessons in our sequence on practicing with the elements of argument are designed to address this problem.

Step 3: Give students opportunities to apply and refine their thinking.

- Repeat the process with the other three teachers, asking students to mark the scales and then do a think-pair-share. Tell students to work with a different classmate on each scale.

- Once again, as students talk, circulate to see what students are saying. If discussions are lagging, prompt them to defend their rating with the Toulmin question "What makes you say so?"

Step 4: Have a whole-class discussion about students' rating.

- Get a sense of the whole by asking how many students rated Mrs. Herzog's claim as the most worth arguing, how many rated Mr. McDonnell's most worth arguing, how many rated Ms. Callahan's most worth arguing, and how many rated Mr. Murdoch's most worth arguing.

- Choose one student and ask him or her to explain why. As you have done before, be consistent using the Toulmin questions "What makes you say so?" and "So what?" to elicit students' reasoning.

- As students are talking, write the criteria they are applying on an anchor chart titled "Characteristics of Effective Claims." For example, a student might say something like "I gave Mrs. Herzog a 2 because it seems to me that she shifts from talking about students to talking about parents. You have to be clear," and you would write "clarity" on the anchor chart. A second student might say something like, "I gave Ms. Callahan a 1 because she doesn't say anything about what should be done. There has to be some kind of action that can be taken," and you would write "action" on the anchor chart.

CLAIMS → Where do you stand?

Sensible/Defensible

Needs to have another side

Clear
Specific

Worth writing about!

People will need to be convinced

- Use follow-up questions to ask students to apply the criteria they articulate. For example, you might say, "Okay, so clarity is important. How do you think the other three teachers fare on that criterion?"

- Continue discussion until students have no new criteria to explain.

Extension: Have students think about a problem at school, brainstorm for potential solutions, and rank the solutions from the most worth arguing to the one least worth arguing. Ask them to write (or present to class) the justifications for their ranking.

Rating Claims

SCENARIO: In recent years, Oxford High School has reported very low academic performances from its students. The ratings for academic performance are based primarily on scores from standardized assessments and overall patterns of student attendance. In response to this dilemma, Principal Jones has asked for input from the faculty. Specifically, he has asked teachers to present him with clear arguments for how to address the situation. Four different teachers have responded.

Read each teacher's argument below. Respond to each argument by marking the scales that follow and writing out an explanation to justify your mark on each scale.

Mrs. Herzog, Math Teacher: Students need to work harder. They sit in class staring at their phones instead of paying attention. They talk over me when I'm trying to teach. Personally, I think it's really the parents who are to blame. The kids in this school obviously don't care about their academics, and there really isn't much teachers can do if the students aren't going to cooperate. We need to start holding the parents more accountable.

Scale A: Mrs. Herzog's claim for how to address the situation is

Mr. McDonnell, Social Studies Teacher: Since the middle schools in the area are also performing poorly, many of our students come into ninth grade without a strong foundation in their academic subjects. We need to develop a peer-to-peer mentoring program where juniors and seniors can tutor the freshman students in their core subjects. I know as a teacher of freshmen that I just don't have enough time in the day to help every student in my class who is falling behind.

Scale B: Mr. McDonnell's claim for how to address the situation is

Ms. Callahan, Spanish Teacher: Just because the scores on the standardized tests are low doesn't mean that the kids in the school are all doing poorly. Many of them just don't care about the test, and they don't give it their best effort. Has anyone even tried to examine the tests closely and figure out what they're really measuring? I see plenty of really bright students come through my classroom each year. I honestly don't think the problem is as bad as the test scores make it seem.

Scale C: Ms. Callahan's claim for how to address the situation is

Mr. Murdoch, Science Teacher: My wife has been teaching at Belmont High School in North Philly for the last 10 years. A few years ago, they were having the same problem in their school. The principal worked together with the teachers to improve the quality of learning taking place in their classrooms. Now, the scores at Belmont have improved considerably over the last few years. I think we should do the same thing here at Oxford.

Scale D: Mr. Murdock's claim for how to address the situation is

1   2   3   4   5   6   7

Not worth arguing   Definitely worth arguing

Nikki seems to confuse Ms. Callahan's warrant for her claim.

Here she contemplates the defensibility of Ms. Callahan's claim through an illustrative example.

She eventually restates the claim.

Here she contemplates the debatability of Ms. Callahan's claim by clarifying the procedures by which the claim can be tested.

Ms. Callahan's claim is definitely worth arguing. She says that the standardized test scores have nothing to do with a student's actual intelligence. Just because a student receives a bad score on a standardized test does not mean that they are particularly not learning anything or exceeding in their academics. Many students receive honor roll all year long, and score low on standardized tests. She thinks that examining the tests will help. I agree that by examining these tests and figuring out what they are measuring and what they should be measuring could help with the situation.

Moving Forward

- We need to reinforce the differences between warrants and claims—in this case, claims have immediate and specific applications, whereas warrants can be applied to a range of circumstances.

- Nikki commits strongly to her mark on the scale. We should work with students on considering how different points on the scales may reflect varying degrees of feasibility for a claim.

What Makes an Effective Claim?

LESSON PLAN

Purpose/Learning Intentions: Understand how a claim should be clear, defensible, and controversial and apply those criteria in evaluating claims.

Length: Approximately 45 minutes

Materials Needed

- A class set of Handout 8.1, "Thinking About College Writing: Ranking Claims"

- A class set of Handout 8.2, "The Marvel of Motordom"

- Copy of yesterday's anchor chart

Lesson Steps

Step 1: Relate this lesson to what has preceded.

- Remind students that in the previous lesson they discussed what made a good claim. Ask a student to reprise the criteria. Refer to the anchor chart developed in the previous lesson.

- Explain that today they're going to apply what they learned yesterday to a situation that all of them will be facing one day in college or technical school: writing in a general education class.

Step 2: Build background knowledge.

- Explain that colleges typically have at least three kinds of courses for graduation: courses in the major, electives, and general education classes. Explain that gen-ed classes typically have two primary purposes: to make sure students get a well-rounded education by having them take classes in a variety of areas and to develop the reading, writing, speaking, and listening skills that they will need to be successful in their majors.

UNIT CONTEXT:

Practicing with the elements of argument

LESSON BACKGROUND:

This is the second lesson of the set of lessons that focus on distinct elements of Toulmin's model. In the last lesson, students discussed the criteria for an effective claim, especially that it be clear and both *defensible* and *controversial*. Here they put that knowledge into action as they evaluate a set of claims in a context that they will face, a general education class. Talking and writing about what makes a good claim should help students develop articulated understandings that they can carry over into their own writing.

- Explain that the class will be pretending to be college students in today's activity.

Step 3: Give students opportunities to apply the criteria for effective claims that they developed.

- Distribute Handouts 8.1 and 8.2.

- Ask students to examine the ad and then rank the claims.

Step 4: Have a whole-class discussion about students' rating.

- Get a sense of the whole by putting a matrix like the following on the board and asking, claim by claim, "How many students gave this claim a 1, 2, 3, 4, 5?"

- Choose the claim about which there is the greatest disagreement. Ask a student who gave it a 1 to explain why. Use the Toulmin probes "What makes you say so?" and "So what?" to help the student elaborate his or her opinion. As students talk, add ideas to the anchor chart as needed.

- Turn to a student who gave the claim a low ranking and repeat the process. Continue to call on students as long as there is energy in the discussion.

- Repeat the process with the other four claims.

	1	2	3	4	5
Claim 1					
Claim 2					
Claim 3					
Claim 4					
Claim 5					

Step 5: Have students apply their understanding to writing.

- Turn students' attention to the writing assignment on Handout 8.1 and ask them to respond to it.

- As they are writing, circulate to provide help as needed.

- Collect their writing as an exit ticket.

Extension: Have students research the general education requirements of a college they might be interested in.

Thinking About College Writing: Ranking Claims

Imagine that you are in a college general education class in U.S. society. As an example, the goals of such classes are similar to the following:

Students will

- Access and analyze historical, analytical, and cultural materials

- Develop observations and conclusions about selected themes in U.S. society and culture

- Construct interpretations using evidence and critical analysis

- Communicate and defend interpretations

- Analyze the ways difference and diversity have shaped the culture and society of the United States

Imagine that it's very early in the semester and your teacher gave you a writing assignment to analyze an ad from 1910. The ad can be found on Handout 8.2. The professor gave you the assignment to see what kind of thinkers she has in class. You really want to get off on the right foot by impressing her.

Rank the following claims from the one that would most likely result in a paper that would make a favorable impression to the one that would be least likely to result in a good paper. Remember, good claims have to be clear, defensible, and controversial.

1. _____ Automobiles have long been very important in American life.

2. _____ A close examination of an automobile ad from 1910 reveals interesting differences between what car buyers cared about then and what they care about now.

3. _____ Automobiles are very different now from what they were in 1910.

4. _____ Times have changed substantially since 1910.

5. _____ An examination of an ad from 1910 reveals that what consumers care about has not dramatically changed in the last century.

Now, write a paragraph in which you explain why you ranked the claims in the order that you did. Justify your choice for the best claim and then explain why each of the other claims is not as good a choice as the one you ranked as #1.

 Available for download at **resources.corwin.com/writersofargument**

The Marvel of Motordom

National Motor Vehicle Company car ad, 1910

JENNIFER
Grade 11

I ranked the claim that there are "interesting differences between what car buyers cared about then vs now" as the best claim because I think that is the most clear on what they are comparing and controversial. The other claims are either not arguable or not clear or deniable. Apart from the last claim which I ranked as 2 because that is almost the counterargument to the first claim, making it controversial and deniable.

> Jennifer shows good awareness of the criteria for an effective claim.

> Although she restated the claim she favors, she gives no specific language from the other claims to show why they are less effective.

> Her observation is astute, but she does not clarify why she chose one claim over the other.

Moving Forward

- We need to continue to work with students to ensure that they are providing enough specific data to address an audience beyond the classroom.

- Jennifer shows awareness of the criteria for an effective claim. We should make sure the other students can do this as well.

What Makes Effective Data? Part 1

UNIT CONTEXT:

Practicing with the elements of argument

LESSON BACKGROUND:

If a claim is both controversial and defensible, it will avoid two conversation-killing responses: "Duh!" (meaning the claim is obvious) or "You're nuts" (meaning your conversational partner doesn't think the claim is defensible). In all other instances, your conversational partner will say something like, "What makes you say so?"—the Toulmin question that gives rise to data. As we explained in Chapter 2, for an argument to advance, your conversational partner has to be willing to stipulate to the data. The following conversation between Jon-Philip, a game aficionado, and Michael, a non-gamer, provides an illustration:

Michael: What game should I get Gabby [Michael's 10-year-old granddaughter] for Christmas?

LESSON PLAN

Purpose/Learning Intentions: Understand that data must be both safe and warrantable. Develop criteria for effective data and test data against those criteria.

Length: Approximately 45 minutes

Materials Needed

- A class set of Handout 9.1, "Thinking About Data"

- Something to record and save students' ideas

Lesson Steps

Step 1: Relate this lesson to what has preceded.

- Remind students that in the previous lessons they discussed what made a good claim. Ask a student to reprise the criteria. Refer to the anchor chart developed in the previous lessons.

- Explain that today the class is moving to work on refining their understanding of another element of an effective argument: data.

- Ask students to recall the question that data answer. They should respond with some version of "What makes you say so?" Note that there are many potential answers to that question and that the effectiveness of their argument will depend in large measure how effective their answer to that question is.

- Explain that today the class will be focusing on *evaluating* data. They're going to apply what they learned yesterday to a situation that all of them will be facing soon: writing for a general education course.

Step 2: Engage students in developing criteria for effective data.

- Distribute Handout 9.1.

- Read the directions and ask students to rank the evidence and write out explanations of their rankings.

Step 3: Have a whole-class discussion about students' ratings.

- As you did last lesson, get a sense of the whole by putting a matrix (see page 84 for an example) on the board and asking, datum by datum, "How many students gave this datum a 1, 2, 3, 4, 5?"

- Choose the piece of data about which there is the greatest disagreement. Ask a student who gave it a 1 to explain why. Use the Toulmin probes "What makes you say so?" and "So what?" to help the student elaborate his or her opinion. As students talk, write ideas on the anchor chart as needed. For example, students will likely address whether the fact in Datum #2 is more persuasive than the story in Datum #3 and whether a foreman is reliably positioned to provide both. So "good source" could then become a criterion for effective data. These criteria for data will be useful for the upcoming lessons as well.

Jon-Philip: Minecraft.

Michael: What makes you say so?

Jon-Philip: It's the best game for kids her age.

Michael: What makes you say so?

Jon-Philip: In Minecraft it's up to the players to set their own goals and, in doing so, to define their own stories.

Michael: So what?

Jon-Philip: Well, you want to foster creativity, don't you?

When Michael asks, "What makes you say so?" in response to Jon-Philip's assertion that Minecraft is the best game for kids, he's really saying, "I don't accept that datum. I need data I can trust before moving on."

Another crucial feature of data is that it has to be warrantable. That is, you have to be able to link it to the claim with a general principle. Jon-Philip does that when he suggests that fostering creativity should be a major criterion in game selection. The purpose of this lesson is to encourage students to think about what data are both safe and warrantable.

Data
What makes you
Say so?

Safe
Good source
Facts (Stories?)
What do they believe? Who are they? What do they Know? Audience will accept
Connectable =
Relates to claim

- Turn to a student who gave the claim low ranking and repeat the process. Continue to call on students as long as there is energy in the discussion.

- Repeat the process with the other five pieces of data.

	1	2	3	4	5
Datum 1					
Datum 2					
Datum 3					
Datum 4					
Datum 5					
Datum 6					

Step 4: Discuss what other data the recommender could have used.

- Have students work in pairs to develop at least one additional piece of data.

- Ask pairs to share their ideas in a whole-class discussion. After they share, ask the groups to test their datum against the criteria the class developed when they discussed their rankings.

Extension: Have students go online and find an argument of some sort. Have them identify each piece of data the writer uses and then rate each piece of data using the following scale:

Thinking About Data

DIRECTIONS: The following letter of recommendation makes an argument using several different types of data. Read the letter carefully. The different types of data have been numbered. When you've finished reading, *rank* the numbered sections of the letter according to how effective you found each type of data. Write out an explanation for each of your rankings.

To Whom It May Concern:

I am writing to recommend Jesse Jones for a job at your manufacturing plant. I was Jesse's immediate supervisor at Lane Industries for 3 years.

(1) During my time at Lane, I have directly supervised over 100 employees. Jesse was certainly among the top 10. (2) During his 3 years at Lane, our productivity went up over 5% each year. (3) Jesse is extremely hard-working. On one occasion, just before Jesse was scheduled to take his vacation, we had a major project due. Although he was leaving the next day, he stayed past midnight to make sure that everything was done and done well. And then while on vacation, he called the plant to check to make sure that everything was delivered on time.

(4) He has other assets as well. One of his co-workers just mentioned to me that Jesse had gone out of his way to explain how to go about filling orders most efficiently and that he would then check in with that co-worker from time to time to make sure she was able to put into practice what Jesse had told her. (5) Jesse is enormously loyal. He's the kind of person who takes pride in his work and always works to the utmost of his ability.

(6) We're very sorry that Jesse is leaving us in order to support his wife who has taken a new job as a school administrator. Indeed, we offered him a substantial raise in the hopes that he would stay. Our loss will be someone else's gain. I offer him my highest recommendation.

Sincerely,

J. P. Imbrenda
Lead Foreman
Lane Industries

 Available for download at **resources.corwin.com/writersofargument**

SASHA
Grade 11

Sasha responds to the task very literally as though her audience includes only those inside the classroom.

She focuses on the content of each piece of data but is less mindful of the differences among the types of data represented.

She demonstrates some awareness of the specific context of the argument by anticipating the needs of its expected audience.

She does not elaborate as to why the data she identifies are irrelevant.

As number one I ranked number 3. I picked 3 as one because it gave examples to why he is a good employee. I ranked 4 as two because it also gave examples of what makes him a good employee but not only that it says he has other assets as well. I ranked 5 as three because it says he's enormously loyal and loyalty is a major aspect in being a good employee. I rank 1 as four because it talks about how he's among the top 10 in being a good employee. I ranked 6 and 2 and the last 2 because they're both sort of irrelevant.

Moving Forward

- In our class discussions, we need to prompt students to attend to the nature of different types of data and how they reflect the demands of different argumentative contexts.

- We should continue to provide paragraph templates to help students internalize the rhetorical features of academic writing that allow it to reach a wide audience.

What Makes Effective Data? Part 2

LESSON PLAN

Purpose/Learning Intentions: Practice identifying data that are both safe and warrantable.

Length: Approximately 45 minutes

Materials Needed

- A class set of Handout 10.1, "More Thinking About Data"

- Yesterday's anchor chart

Lesson Steps

Step 1: Relate this lesson to what has preceded.

- Remind students that yesterday they considered what makes effective data.

- Turn to the anchor chart and ask students to explain what each item means and to provide an example.

- Explain that today the class is going to get more practice in applying those criteria and that they'll be thinking about how, if at all, those criteria vary from audience to audience. In the previous lesson, we mentioned how, as students developed criteria for effective data, future lessons would give them opportunities to think about how those criteria might vary across different contexts and types of arguments. Remind them that this kind of thinking will be a key part of the lesson.

Step 2: Engage students in applying criteria for data.

- Distribute Handout 10.1.

- Have students rank the data from all three scenarios, but ask them not to write out explanations just yet.

UNIT CONTEXT:

Practicing with the elements of argument

LESSON BACKGROUND:

This lesson will give students more practice in applying the criteria for effective data that they developed during the last class. In addition, it is designed to engage students in understanding that data are of varying types, and the effectiveness of those types is at least in part a function of the audience.

Jon-Philip's dissertation research is an analysis of the impact of the instructional intervention from which our lessons are drawn. We shared the finding that our instruction significantly improved students' scores on a college-placement writing task. Jon-Philip did qualitative analyses as well. Perhaps the most interesting of these is his noticing that students tended to label texts as one of two broad types: (1) enumerated facts, and (2) elaborated opinions. This lesson is designed to

(Continued)

add some nuance to that categorization by having students consider the power of short narratives, which they often thought of as mere opinion, and to choose among pieces of numerical data to determine which provides the safest and most warrantable starting point.

Step 3: Have small-group discussions about students' ratings.

- Divide class into six small groups. Assign two groups to discuss their ratings of one of the scenarios. That is, two groups should discuss Scenario A, two groups should discuss Scenario B, and two groups should discuss Scenario C. Circulate as the small groups are discussing.

- Pair members from one of the two groups that discussed Scenario A with a counterpart from the other group that discussed Scenario A. Create similar pairings for the groups that discussed Scenarios B and C. Tell pairs that they should discuss their rankings and that they should write their rationale for their rankings during/after the paired discussion.

Step 4: Have a whole-class discussion of the rankings.

- Ask students who discussed Scenario A to share their rankings. Probe for their rationales. Make sure that you ask about how, if at all, the nature of the audience affected their rankings. Refer to the anchor chart from yesterday's lesson. Add or qualify items on the chart as needed. For example, when discussing Scenario B, you might explain to students that the criterion of facts from a good source from the previous lesson may not be as important in an informal argument between two friends as it would be in a more formal argument that could result in a new policy that will affect many people.

- Repeat the process for the other two scenarios.

Step 5: Remind students to apply what they have learned when crafting their own arguments.

Extension: Have students work in pairs, with one member writing an argument about an issue to one audience and the other member writing about the same claim to a different audience. Have them explain the extent to which their audience determined the data that they used.

More Thinking About Data

DIRECTIONS: Each of the scenarios below involves an argument someone might make to a particular audience. For each *claim*, there are four pieces of *data* that might be used to support it. Rank the four pieces of *data* and *then write out a brief explanation of your rankings.* Justify why the *data* you ranked as #1 are the best, and then explain why the other pieces of *data* are not as strong.

Scenario A

CLAIM: Mr. Jay should not be allowed to teach high school.

AUDIENCE: School principal

DATA:

_____ (1) He gives way too much homework.

_____ (2) One student of his explains: "I went to see him after school for extra help three times. The first time, he yelled at me for bothering him. The second time, he left after only 5 minutes because he said he had something more important to do. The third time he stayed and worked with me, but he made fun of me the whole time, calling me stupid because I couldn't keep up in class."

_____ (3) Last year, 10% of his students failed his classes.

_____ (4) His lessons are so boring that half of the students fall asleep during his class.

Scenario B

CLAIM: We should eat dinner at McDonald's tonight.

AUDIENCE: A friend who prefers Burger King over McDonald's

DATA:

_____ (1) McDonald's is the world's largest chain of fast food restaurants, serving around 68 million customers every day across 119 countries.

_____ (2) The last time I ate at Burger King, I had to wait in line for more than 10 minutes before I got my food.

_____ (3) In a blind taste test, 62% of people preferred the Big Mac over the Whopper.

_____ (4) Unlike Burger King, McDonald's serves breakfast all day.

(Continued)

Scenario C

CLAIM: The United States Congress *should not* pass a law banning private ownership of handguns.

AUDIENCE: United States Congress

DATA:

_____ (1) A National Rifle Association self-defense pamphlet reads: "Literally tens of millions of Americans disapprove of banning private ownership of handguns."

_____ (2) The Second Amendment guarantees all citizens the right to bear arms.

_____ (3) A study of state prisoners found that 56% of the inmates agreed that a criminal would be much less likely to approach a victim if he or she knew the victim was armed with a gun. Seventy-four percent of the prisoners agreed that criminals avoid houses when people are home because they fear being shot.

_____ (4) According to a recent poll, 1 out of every 5 American males fears that himself or a close loved one will be the victim of a terrorist attack.

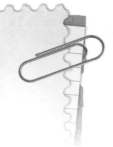

Scenario B: I ranked 3 as number 1 because a blind taste test can say a lot because everyone is getting to taste the same thing. I ranked 1 as number 4 because just because it's been around for a long time does not mean it's still the same. For example, my local supermarket has been around for a long time and my grandmother says all the time that the supermarket is not the same any more. I ranked 4 as number 2 because it only matters if you're trying to get breakfast. Lastly, I ranked 2 as number 3 because you can't just go on one experience.

> *Chris demonstrates an understanding of the persuasive power of data that is empirical in nature.*

> *He is right to identify that the particular piece of data is not relevant to the argument, but he misreads the data.*

> *He shows a concern for the relevance of a particular data point to the context of the argument.*

> *He suggests a conceptual understanding of the danger of making generalizations from a single instance.*

Moving Forward

- Chris demonstrates a range of implicit criteria to govern the effectiveness of data in a particular context. We should work with students to make those criteria more explicit and to generate principles that reflect the criteria.

- We have to keep pushing students to write for an audience beyond the classroom. We should provide paragraph templates more consistently.

How Do Warrants Relate to Claims and Data?

UNIT CONTEXT:

Elements of argument. The lesson could also be used to introduce an inquiry unit built around some version of the question "What makes good learning and teaching?"

LESSON BACKGROUND:

As you recall from our introductory chapters and our previous lessons, effective arguments articulate the general principles that connect the data to the claim or claims. Think back to the little argument we shared in the Lesson Background to Lesson 9. It doesn't matter that Minecraft requires players to set their own goals, allowing them to define their own stories unless that's something 10-year-olds like and profit from.

The purpose of this lesson is to engage students in a ranking activity that requires them to articulate warrants. We use scenarios related to learning as we think that students have tacit understandings of their position on that issue.

LESSON PLAN

Purpose/Learning Intentions: Produce warrants for claims you make about what makes good learning, in doing so, connecting data to claims.

Length: Approximately 45 minutes

Materials Needed

- A class set of Handout 11.1, "What Makes Good Learning?"

- Something to record and save students' ideas

Lesson Steps

Step 1: Relate this lesson to what has preceded.

- Remind students that the class has talked about how effective data have to provide a safe starting point and have to be something that clearly connects to the claim.

  → Recall that that connection is the answer to the "So what?" question and that we've called the connection a "warrant."

  → Recall that answers to the "so what?" question need to state general principles, ones that can work both in the particular argument that someone is making as well as similar situations.

- Explain that today the class will be working on an activity designed to encourage them to create warrants for arguments that relate to a very important question: "What makes good learning?"

Step 2: Leverage students' background knowledge.

- Ask students to write for 5 minutes on the following prompt. Tell them that they will be sharing their responses with a partner.

→ Think about a time when you felt you had a really effective learning experience. It could have come at school, but it doesn't have to have. You could also think about something that occurred outside school, maybe at home or work or while you were participating in one of your favorite out-of-school activities. Explain as best you can what you learned and how you learned it.

- Have students share their writing in pairs.

Step 3: Engage students in producing warrants for the claims they make about what makes good learning.

- Distribute Handout 11.1.

- Tell students to keep in mind what they and their partner wrote as you read the four scenarios.

- Read the scenes aloud.

- Give students 5 minutes or so to rank the quality of the learning experiences.

Step 4: Lead a whole-class discussion of students' rankings.

- As you have done in the other ranking activities, get a sense of the whole by putting a matrix like the following on the board and asking, "How many of you gave this scenario a 1, 2, 3, 4?"

- Choose the scenario about which there is the greatest disagreement. Ask a student who gave it a 1 to explain why. Use the Toulmin probes "What makes you say so?" and "So what?" If students don't articulate a general rule say, "And the general rule is?" to help the student elaborate his or her opinion. As students talk, write ideas on the anchor chart as needed. For example, a student might say, "I ranked Shantelle as #1 because she got to the point where she could play perfectly." Then, you might help that student to articulate a general rule about learning such as, "Effective learning means getting as good as one can possibly get at something." We really enjoy helping students to articulate these kinds of rules because, while the statement itself is certainly reasonable, it also allows for a good amount of healthy disagreement from other students who may prefer to think of effective learning in a very different way.

- Turn to a student who gave the scenario a low ranking and repeat the process. Continue to call on students as long as there is energy in the discussion.

- Repeat the process with the other three scenarios.

After all, in order to complain about or praise a class, one would have to, and that's something we know students like to do!

	1	2	3	4
Tommy				
Melinda				
Frankie				
Shantelle				

Step 5: Discuss students' justifications for their rankings.

- Once the discussion is complete, give students a chance to re-examine their initial rankings and write their justifications. Circulate as they write. If students aren't writing general rules, encourage them to do so.

- Ask students to read their justifications, or general rules. Ask for volunteers to read until the justifications are becoming repetitious.

- Ask students what they learned about warrants and how to write them. Record their observations on the anchor chart.

Warrants =
So what?

- Builds a bridge
  data — claim

- General rule → May have to explain how it works
  Applies to more than one situation
  Can't be too big
  May have to qualify (mostly......)
  People have used the rule before

Extension: Have students write a new scenario that they would rank as #2. Have them explain how their scenario illustrates a general principle that they have about learning.

What Makes Good Learning?

DIRECTIONS: Rank the main character in each of the following stories according to the quality of learning each one experienced. Give a 1 to the character you think had the highest quality learning experience, all the way through to a 4 for the character you think had the lowest quality experience. Then, write a paragraph explaining your rankings. Justify your choice for the #1 learning experience and explain why each of the others was not as high in quality.

_____ Tommy has had the same baseball coach, Coach Davis, throughout his last 3 years of high school. Coach Davis has worked closely with him to improve his swing. All of the players know that Coach Davis's approach to batting is based on his four key principles. Tommy, like most of the players, knows the four principles so well he can recite them without even thinking about it. However, Tommy isn't always great at putting the principles into practice. Although his batting average has gone up, he's still only hitting at around .250, which isn't much of an improvement from his freshman year when he was hitting around .230.

_____ Melinda has just accepted her first job at a prestigious software design firm. During her job interview, her new boss asked her why she wanted to be a software designer. At first, Melinda wasn't sure how to answer the question—she'd set herself onto the path several years ago and hadn't really thought much about it since. But then she started to think back to her tenth-grade geometry class. To be honest, she couldn't remember much about the class itself. Software design doesn't involve very much geometry. She just remembered how inspiring her teacher was, and how it was the first time in her life she felt passionate about math. For Melinda, that geometry class was the experience that set her on the path to where she is today.

_____ When Frankie first started working at his brother Bill's auto shop, he knew nothing about cars. Bill wasn't much for explaining things, but he would let Frankie watch what he was doing, and he would always give Frankie a chance to try things for himself. Frankie quickly learned how to do a lot of the day-to-day things around the shop on his own. He could change oil and brake fluid, rotate tires, and replace headlights and windshield wipers. One day, the shop was really busy, and Bill asked Frankie to install new brakes on a car that had just come in. Although Frankie had watched Bill install brakes before, he'd never tried it himself, and he was a little unsure of how to get started. Frankie pulled the car onto the lift and started to raise it up when he felt a sudden thump against the side of his head. He turned to find Bill sneering angrily at him. In a few stern words, Bill explained to Frankie that he hadn't set the car fully into place before he started raising the lift. Suffice to say, Frankie never made that mistake again.

_____ Shantelle has a piano competition coming up soon. Her teacher has gone through the piece she will be performing with her several times, note by note, explaining every detail. Her teacher has also recorded the piece the way it should be played. Shantelle listens to it all the time; she even falls asleep with her headphones on and the song playing on repeat. Shantelle practices hours every day—so many hours that her friends and family begin to worry about her, and everything else in her life has become second to piano practice. Eventually, she is able to play the piece just as perfectly as her teacher. When the day of the competition finally arrives, Shantelle performs the piece just as well as she'd hoped. In fact, she was surprised at how easily it just came to her. She won first place at the competition, and her dream of becoming a professional piano player seemed a little bit more within her reach.

 Available for download at **resources.corwin.com/writersofargument**

Nikki realizes that some readers may not be familiar with the scenario. Her claim comes in conjunction with a short summary of her data.

She makes her warrant explicit. Now, she has to use this principle as a criterion for comparison.

Her criterion of hands-on learning is implied here.

Another statement to explain the principle behind this reasoning would strengthen Nikki's argument.

Nikki strays from her initial warrant at the end here. Mimicking is not clearly related to her earlier principle about hands-on learning.

I think that Frankie had the best learning experience. He started working at his brother's auto shop with no knowledge about cars at all. As he continued working with his brother in his auto shop, he began to learn things. He was getting a hands-on learning experience. He made a mistake and thanks to Bill he would never make that mistake again. Having a hands-on experience gives you a better learning experience. I ranked the others lower than Frankie, because they did not learn as much as Frankie did. Tommy gained knowledge, but he did not apply it to improve his batting average. Shantelle learned how to perfect her piano piece and was satisfied with her outcome. However, I do not think that her experience was the best learning experience, because she was just mimicking what she was taught. Finally, Melinda got a positive outcome from a class that she did not remember anything about. She gained her passion for what she does based off of a teacher from a class that she has no recollection of.

Moving Forward

- Nikki sets up a strong argument, but her reasoning is not consistent all the way through. We need to work with the students in getting them to apply their warrants as consistent criteria across examples.

- Comparing problematized scenarios is working well in helping students to understand the relationships among claims, data, and warrants.

Practice Writing Warrants

LESSON PLAN

Purpose/Learning Intentions: Articulate warrants in order to connect data to claims.

Length: Approximately 30 minutes

Materials Needed

- A class set of Handout 12.1, "More Work With Warrants"

- Yesterday's anchor chart

Lesson Steps

Step 1: Relate this lesson to what has preceded.

- Remind students that in yesterday's discussion, the facts of each of the cases were not under dispute, so the whole argument hinged on the *warrant*, the general principles about learning that they applied to the facts in order to do their ranking.

- Explain that in today's class they are going to get more practice in writing warrants.

- Direct students' attention to the anchor chart from the previous lesson. Ask volunteers to explain each item on it.

Step 2: Engage students in writing warrants.

- Distribute Handout 12.1.

- Read Argument A. Ask students to write a warrant for the argument. Give them a couple of minutes to do so. As they write, circulate and read over their shoulders, pushing them to frame their warrant as a general principle as needed.

UNIT CONTEXT:

Elements of argument

LESSON BACKGROUND:

Throughout his career, Michael (cf. Smith, 2007) has been extolling the power of practice in miniature. Practice in miniature provides students with targeted opportunities to apply what they have learned. Warrants are difficult to write, so it's important to provide ample opportunities to do so. You'll notice in the little writing exercise that composes this lesson we ask students to practice writing warrants that connect different kinds of data to everyday claims.

One of the things we noticed when we taught this lesson is that students sometimes tended to restate claims instead of producing warrants that explain how a claim connects to data. For example, when considering the first argument on the handout—

(Continued)

> *Kareem Abdul-Jabbar is the greatest basketball player of all time. He scored 38,387 points throughout his career, more than any other player in NBA history.*

—a student might write, "You have to be great to score that many points." That's close, but not quite there. A warrant that more clearly articulates the general rule or principle at work would be something like the following: "Winning basketball requires teams to outscore their opponents, so scoring ability is the truest sign of greatness." Not a huge difference, we know, but it will be important to push students to write principles that apply beyond the particular scenario.

- Ask several volunteers to read their warrants. It's likely that they will closely resemble each other, so stop requesting volunteers when they become repetitive. For instance, students might respond to Argument A by writing, "The best basketball players are the ones who can score the most points," or "Scoring points is the most important quality of a great basketball player." At that point, you can stop and explain how the warrants enacted the criteria on the anchor chart.

- Have students work individually on the other four arguments. Once again, circulate as they are writing to provide praise and support as needed.

Step 3: Have students share their writing in small groups.

- Divide the class into groups of four or five.

- Have students share their warrants in the small groups.

- Ask each group to select the warrant that they think is the best for each of the arguments. Explain that you will be asking them to share their selection to the whole class along with the rationale for their choice.

Step 4: Have a whole-class discussion of warrants.

- Have each group share its selection for Argument 2 and explain why they made their choice. Add any new insights from these explanations to the anchor chart.

- Have similar discussions around the other three arguments.

Extension: Explain that the arguments on the handout are only skeletons of complete arguments. Have them select one of the arguments and elaborate it into a fully developed paragraph.

More Work With Warrants

DIRECTIONS: Each of the arguments below has a *claim* and some *data* but no *warrant*. Add a warrant to each one.

Argument A: Kareem Abdul-Jabbar is the greatest basketball player of all time. He scored 38,387 points throughout his career, more than any other player in NBA history.

Argument B: Pat Tillman is a true hero. After the terrorist attacks on September 11, 2001, he gave up his career in the NFL and joined the Army.

Argument C: It was a terrible decision to buy an Android phone instead of an iPhone. I've had the Android for a week now, and I still can't figure out how to use it.

Argument D: My sister is the smartest person I know. It's now her senior year in high school, and she has never received a grade lower than an A− in any of her classes.

Argument E: The United States Supreme Court should ban the death penalty. Since 1989, 337 people on death row have been exonerated due to DNA evidence.

 Available for download at **resources.corwin.com/writersofargument**

MARIO
Grade 11

Mario veers away from the directions here, providing a warrant that actually counters the claim from the prompt. The warrant he provides, however, does successfully refute the claim.

Mario's shift into the rhetorical "you" here weakens his academic voice.

Mario's underlying principles hint at his no-nonsense personal value system.

His warrant here seems to be merely restating the claim. We're not sure he sees the controversial nature of this topic.

Again, Mario has presented a claim instead of a warrant. A warrant would reflect a more general concern for how the trial-by-jury system has proven to be unreliable at times.

A: In order to be the best at something you have to have the best record of all time.

B: Just because you give up everything in your life to do something heroic, it does not mean you're a hero.

C: Don't buy something you have no idea how to use then complain about it. You should stick to what you know how to use.

D: In order to be the smartest person you know you have to always maintain your grades high.

E: Never give someone a penalty without full evidence.

Moving Forward

- Students show progress in distinguishing between claims and warrants, but they still need more practice across a range of different kinds of arguments.

- Mario, like many of our students, has a strong and consistent set of personal values that he applies to his argumentative reasoning. We should work with students in thinking about how some values are more valuable than others in academic settings.

Notes

_____

_____

_____

_____

_____

_____

_____

_____

_____

_____

_____

_____

_____

_____

Chapter 6

Applying What They've Learned About Argument to Texts

The heart of most English language arts classes with which we're familiar is the teaching of texts, and we realize that many teachers won't take up the ideas that we're sharing unless they are useful in thinking about the teaching of texts. In this chapter, we share lessons focusing on four different kinds of texts:

- Simulated texts
- Literary texts
- Narrative nonfiction texts
- Disciplinary nonfiction texts

Who Is Going to Bounce Back?

LESSON PLAN

Purpose/Learning Intentions: Through use of a ranking activity, learn how thinking about resilience requires us to consider the nature of a setback and the resources the person who faced the setback can draw upon. Use all of the elements of Toulmin's model in crafting an argument.

Length: Approximately 45 minutes

Materials Needed

- A class set of Handout 13.1, "Who Will Bounce Back?"

- Something to record and save students' ideas

Lesson Steps

Step 1: Introduce the lesson.

- Explain to students that this lesson will kick off the class's investigation of another essential question: "What makes someone resilient?" Explain that resilience is the term for someone who is able to bounce back from some kind of setback.

- Remind students that any complex question has lots of potential answers, so they'll have to be persuasive in making their cases. Note that this means they need to make a claim that's clear, defensible, and controversial, support that claim with evidence that provides a safe starting point, and connect the data to the claim with a warrant.

Step 2: Leverage students' background knowledge.

- Ask students to write for 5 minutes on the following prompt. Tell them that they will be sharing their responses with a partner.

  → Think about someone you know who faced a setback of one sort or another and was able to bounce back from that setback. It could be

The first lesson of the "What makes someone resilient?" unit. This lesson will introduce the question, while the next four lessons in this chapter will examine it further through a variety of texts. You can also use it as a stand-alone lesson.

LESSON BACKGROUND:

When we develop a unit around an essential question, one of the first steps we take is to think about the dimensions of the question. That is, we want to think specifically about the issues that sustain the cultural conversation around the essential question. When we thought about the question "What makes someone resilient?" we identified two distinct dimensions:

1. From what does someone have to bounce back?

2. What resources are available to help the person bounce back?

(Continued)

LESSON BACKGROUND:
(Continued)

In the simulated texts that follow, you'll see we manipulated those two dimensions of the larger question. Each scenario focuses on a different setback: physical injury, personal loss, economic reversal, and a larger cultural setback. In each scenario, the main characters have different resources. Some characters have family support, others don't. Some have the support of friends, others don't. Some have some kind of institutional support, and others don't. Discussing the scenarios should set the stage for investigating the complex question even as it requires students to produce fully formed arguments.

You'll note that the approach we take in this lesson is very much like the one we took in our other ranking activities. If you're worried that your students might find the lessons too repetitive, don't be. We found that students are very willing to engage in the kinds of conversations the ranking lessons foster.

someone you know personally or a fictional character that you've read about or seen. Explain what setback the person faced, and why you think he or she was able to bounce back.

- Have students share their writing in pairs.

Step 3: Engage students in the ranking activity.

- Tell students to keep in mind what they and their partner wrote as you read the four scenarios.

- Pass out the handout and then read the scenarios aloud.

- Give students 5 minutes or so to do their rankings.

Step 4: Have small-group discussions of students' rankings.

- Divide students into groups of four or five to discuss their rankings. Explain that you're not asking them to come to a consensus, but rather to explain their thinking to each other.

- Circulate as groups are talking. Encourage students who are not speaking by noting their rankings and saying something like "I see you disagree. What makes you say so?" Use other Toulmin prompts as needed.

Step 5: Lead a whole-class discussion of students' rankings.

- As you have done in the other ranking activities, get a sense of the whole by putting a matrix like the following on the board and asking, "How many of you gave this scenario a 1, 2, 3, 4?"

- Choose the scenario about which there is the greatest disagreement. Ask a student who gave it a 1 to explain why. Use the Toulmin probes "What makes you say so?" and "So what?" to help the student elaborate his or her opinion. As students talk, write ideas on the anchor chart as needed.

- Turn to a student who gave the scenario a low ranking and repeat the process. Continue to call on students as long as there is energy in the discussion.

- Repeat the process with the other three scenarios.

	1	2	3	4
Tiara				
Matias				
Juliet				
Malik				

Step 6: Have students write their justifications in a short paragraph.

- Once the discussion is complete, ask students to write out their justifications. Circulate as they write. As you circulate, encourage students to elaborate by using the Toulmin questions, and by reminding them that there were lots of different opinions, so they need to be persuasive.

- Collect justifications as an exit ticket.

Extension: Have students choose a celebrity who has suffered a reversal and ask them to write a paragraph in which they explain what reversal the celebrity suffered, whether they think the celebrity will bounce back, and what they base their prediction on.

Who Will Bounce Back?

DIRECTIONS: When some people suffer a setback, they are able to bounce back. When other people suffer a setback, it seems to defeat them. The ability to bounce back is called *resilience*. In this unit, we're going to examine the question "What makes people resilient?" We're starting our investigation of that question by considering the scenes below.

Please read each scenario and then *rank them from the person most likely to be able to bounce back* (1) to the person least likely to be able to bounce back (4). Then, write a short paragraph in which you explain your top pick.

_____ **1.** Everything seemed to be going great for Tiara. That is, everything was going great until the injury. Star basketball player. Straight A student. Things had always come pretty easily to Tiara. Sure, things were a little rough at home. Tiara really didn't get along with her mom. Tiara's mom was really religious. It seemed to Tiara that all her mom cared about was the church. She'd come home from basketball practice tired and hungry, and there'd be no dinner, just a note saying her mom was at services and she should find something to eat. But that was okay because basketball made everything worthwhile. Tiara was all-city as a sophomore. College recruiters from UConn, Duke, and Stanford had already been to see her. Now, Tiara lay in a hospital bed recovering from microfracture surgery, the same surgery that had ended the careers of Penny Hardaway, Chris Webber, and Tracy McGrady, three NBA superstars. The other girls on the team had all texted her pledging that they would help in whatever way they could. Her coach had already stopped by and told her that she'd help in whatever way she could in rehabbing the injury. The coach told Tiara that she'd always have her brains to fall back on if her body let her down. Tiara knew it was a joke, but she wondered why she should try at anything if it could be so easily taken away. And her mom said the injury was a sign from God that Tiara should be spending less time at practice and more time at church. "I'll show her," Tiara thought. But she wondered if she really would.

_____ **2.** Whatever happened, Matias knew, his grandmother would always be there for him. Matias's mom and dad both worked two jobs trying to save money for his and his sister's college funds. He knows they love him, but they have never been around much. But his grandmom—his grandmom was his rock. She watched out for him. He'll never forget the time when she chased away some gang members from the playground in order to protect him. Or all the time she spent reading to him. Or how she came to every single soccer game he ever played, from peewee leagues to high school. Matias was a good student. Not straight As, but he always did his best. He'd never risk disappointing his grandmother. That's why when he heard that she had pancreatic cancer it hit him so hard. Pancreatic cancer, the fastest cancer there is. He'd barely have enough time to say a proper good bye. He didn't know how he'd be able to continue without her. "Why me?" Matias thought. He didn't have any friends close enough to share his pain. His parents tried to comfort him, but he found it hard to talk with them. He found himself having trouble sleeping, and his attention drifted away in class. Mr. Nelson, his English teacher, noticed, and tried to talk with him. But Matias started crying in their after-school meeting, and now he's embarrassed to go back and see him again. Matias knows the kind of life his grandmother would want for him, but he's not sure he can get there without her.

_____ **3.** Juliet loved working at the family body shop. Ever since she was a little girl, she'd go and watch her dad and now her brothers make miracles out of wrecks of cars. Every detail was always perfect. Little wonder the shop was so successful. Juliet and her mom would take care of the books, while her dad and her brothers worked. In fact, Juliet had become something of a whiz in math. She was great at the calculations, and that got her interested in higher math as well. Her dad said he wanted her to be the first in the family to go to college. And not just any college. He wanted her to shoot for MIT, maybe the best college in the country for someone who wanted to be an engineer, the job Juliet had wanted since she was a tiny girl building with Legos. She had the grades and the scores to make it, and the family had put away enough money that they could swing tuition if she didn't get a scholarship. But all that changed in a flash. One of the cars they worked on was in another accident right after it left the shop. The driver was seriously injured and claimed that it was because of faulty repairs. And despite lots of evidence to the contrary, the jury agreed. Of course, the shop had insurance, but not enough to cover the loss. Juliet's college fund had to go to pay the settlement, and they'd be paying off the remainder with their profits for the next 10 years. MIT was now just a dream. She got accepted, but didn't get close to enough money to make it affordable. It would be hard enough to pay community college tuition, especially since word of the lawsuit slowed business way down. Juliet still loved going to the shop to be with her family, and she still loved to see the work—when there was any. But she could see that the problems with the business were eating away at her dad. He'd started drinking and his eyes didn't have that same brightness anymore. She could understand why. She heard whispers that some people thought her family had gotten what they deserved, that they had become too big for their own britches, as the saying goes. That was hard to take and Juliet wondered if the people she thought were friends felt that way. And what's worse, Juliet had to face the fact that she'd have to give up her dream. Being a bookkeeper wasn't such a bad thing. But it wasn't the same as being an engineer. Not by a long shot.

_____ 4. Growing up in his neighborhood, Malik didn't have many encounters with White people. Not many good ones anyway. The teachers in his charter school were mostly Black or Latinx, and all the kids were as well. So it was quite a shock when they moved to the suburbs, supposedly for a better education. For the first time in his life, Malik knew what it felt like to be in the minority. Only about 10% of the students were of color and almost none of the teachers were. Malik and his family moved to get a better education, but it wasn't better for Malik. Nothing he did was good enough. Nothing he said was correct enough. For the first time in his life, Malik was on academic probation. And it wasn't his fault, he thought. When he tried to talk about his situation at home, his mom and dad weren't very sympathetic. His dad just got promoted at work by his White boss, and his mom was a nurse who had always worked for a White doctor. His dad would say that Malik was just using the race issue as an excuse and would harp on him about working harder so that he would be above reproach. Sometimes Malik would think about giving it a try. But then there'd be the news of Michael Brown, or Tamir Rice. Walter Scott was the last straw. His murder really sent Malik into a tailspin. His grades got worse and worse. But, Malik thought, what difference did it make? The cards were stacked against him, so why even try?

By signaling back to the source of her data, Corona makes a move common to academic discourse.

Corona treats this claim as though it is a widely accepted belief. A reader may not necessarily agree.

She implies that the support he receives from others is what gives Matias the strength to bounce back, but her reasoning is not explicit.

Out of the four people I read about, I think Matias has the best chance at bouncing back. Even though he is sad about losing his grandmother, he already has her deep inside his heart. The kind of strength you can get from people who care about you stays with you even after the people are gone. I should know. Now, Matias still has even more people looking out for him so as soon as he gets passed the first few weeks and starts to move on from his grandmother's loss, he will be able to go back to the person he was before.

Moving Forward

- Ranking scenarios has again proven to provide students with an accessible way to generate very complex reasoning.

- While her reasoning is strong, Corona focuses only on the scenario she ranked as #1. We have to guide students in how to make inferences across a range of scenarios.

Using Three Key Questions to Understand a Poem

LESSON PLAN

Purpose/Learning Intentions: Apply what you have learned about argumentation to writing a literary argument, using three key questions to help you understand a poem.

Length: Approximately 75 minutes in one block or over two classes

Materials Needed

- Four greeting cards, two from each of two occasions with different perspectives (e.g., a brother and a sister)

- A class set of Handout 14.1, "If" by Rudyard Kipling

Lesson Steps

Step 1: Give a mini-lesson on understanding the rhetorical situation of a poem.

- Display two greeting cards on the same occasion but written from different perspectives. For example, you might bring in a birthday card to a sister from the perspective of a brother and another card written from the perspective of a sister to a sister.

- Have a whole-class discussion on how the cards are similar and different. For example, the sister-to-sister card might suggest shared understandings that the brother-to-sister card does not.

- Display the other pair of cards, for example, a Mother's Day card from a grandchild and then one from a son or daughter.

- Once again, have a whole-class discussion on the similarities and differences in the cards.

UNIT CONTEXT:

What makes someone resilient?

LESSON BACKGROUND:

Thus far our focus has been primarily on everyday arguments, and the texts that we have introduced have been nonfiction or little narratives that we have devised. We realize, however, that in most English classes, students write the bulk of their arguments about literature. This lesson and the one that follows illustrate how we would approach such instruction within the context of a unit.

You'll see in this lesson three principles that guide our instruction:

1. *We introduce the literature in the context of an inquiry unit built around an essential question*, in this case, what makes someone resilient. The readings that students did in this unit focused on two distinct aspects of the question.

(Continued)

- From what does the person have to bounce back (e.g., a physical setback, economic reversal, personal disappointment)?

- Upon what resources can a person draw (e.g., personal strength, the support of family or friends, the support of some institution or the community, faith)?

2. *We begin the lesson with a mini-lesson on a reading strategy that is transferable to other texts. As we argued in our introductory chapters, transfer is crucially important. The reading and writing that we ask students to do should be preparing them for their future reading, writing, or thinking. No reading or writing that students do is very important unless it has that future focus.*

3. *We want students to see themselves as authorized to disagree with what characters, speakers, and authors say or think. That is, we want them to see literature not just as something to be interpreted, but also as something to be contended with, a point Michael elaborates in* Authorizing Readers *(Rabinowitz & Smith, 1998).*

- Explain that we should do the same kind of thinking whenever we read poems and ask "Who is the speaker? Who is the audience? What is the occasion?"

Step 2: Have a whole-class discussion of the poem.

- Distribute Handout 14.1.

- Read the poem aloud, pausing afterward to define any words your students might find unfamiliar (e.g., "knaves" or "pitch and toss").

- Upon completing the reading, ask students to discuss the three key questions:

  → Who is the speaker?

  → Who is the audience?

  → What is the occasion?

- Move stanza by stanza to make sure that students have a literal understanding of the poem. Ask:

  → Let's look at the first stanza. Can you tell me a situation that would cause people to lose their head? How might someone behave in the situation if he or she had not lost it?

  → What would it mean if someone had made dreams his or her master?

  → What might the game of pitch-and-toss represent?

  → What does the speaker think might happen if someone walks with crowds or with Kings?

Step 3: Have students complete and discuss the two resilience scales.

- Give students 3 minutes or so to complete the scales.

- While they are doing so, draw each of the scales on the board or some chart paper.

- Tally responses by asking, "How many put it all the way over to within yourself?"

- Move point by point until you have moved through all of the scale points. (It's likely that students' responses will cluster on the left side of the scale.) Ask students to explain their ratings, making sure to use the Toulmin questions:

  → Where do you stand?

  → What makes you say so?

  → So what?

- Lead a similar discussion with Scale 2.

Step 4: Have students write a critique of the speaker's position.

- Explain that any literary text is a turn in an ongoing conversation. Note that it's important to use texts to help them think and that one way to do so is to disagree.

- Explain that you want them to examine their own lives or lives that they have read about or learned about in films and movies and to consider to what extent their experience challenges the position of the speaker.

- As students plan and write, circulate. You may have to help students get started by asking them to tell you a story about someone they know about who has faced an obstacle. Explain that in their writing, they will need to make a claim about the likelihood that a person will be able to bounce back. They will use the life of the person they have chosen as data to support that claim.

Step 5: Have students share their writing in pairs.

- Divide students in pairs to share what they have written.

- Have partners ask these questions of their partner's writing:

  → Is the claim clearly stated and both defensible and controversial?

  → Do the data provide a safe starting point? Are they sufficiently explained so that the audience can understand them?

  → Does the author connect the data and claim with a warrant? Does the warrant provide a general principle that can be applied beyond the specific situation?

Extension: Have students find parodies of "If" online and to identify the speaker, audience, occasion, and main idea of the parody.

"If" by Rudyard Kipling

If you can keep your head when all about you
Are losing theirs and blaming it on you,
If you can trust yourself when all men doubt you,
But make allowance for their doubting too;
If you can wait and not be tired by waiting,
Or being lied about, don't deal in lies,
Or being hated, don't give way to hating,
And yet don't look too good, nor talk too wise:

If you can dream—and not make dreams your master;
If you can think—and not make thoughts your aim;
If you can meet with Triumph and Disaster
And treat those two impostors just the same;
If you can bear to hear the truth you've spoken
Twisted by knaves to make a trap for fools,
Or watch the things you gave your life to, broken,
And stoop and build 'em up with worn-out tools:

If you can make one heap of all your winnings
And risk it on one turn of pitch-and-toss,
And lose, and start again at your beginnings
And never breathe a word about your loss;
If you can force your heart and nerve and sinew
To serve your turn long after they are gone,
And so hold on when there is nothing in you
Except the Will which says to them: 'Hold on!'

If you can talk with crowds and keep your virtue,
Or walk with Kings—nor lose the common touch,
If neither foes nor loving friends can hurt you,
If all men count with you, but none too much;
If you can fill the unforgiving minute
With sixty seconds' worth of distance run,
Yours is the Earth and everything that's in it,
And—which is more—you'll be a Man, my son!

Scale A: The speaker of the poem believes that resilience primarily comes from

1 2 3 4 5 6 7

Within yourself   Others around you

Scale B: The speaker of the poem argues that overcoming setbacks is

1 2 3 4 5 6 7

Always easy   Never easy

Writing Portfolio

Compose a brief counterargument to the author's stance on resilience. To do so, you should make a claim that goes against how you marked Scale B above and then support that claim through personal experience and good reasoning. Don't forget to include a "So what?" statement that provides a more general principle about what it is that makes someone resilient! Your counterargument should be one well-developed paragraph.

 Available for download at **resources.corwin.com/writersofargument**

> *By disputing the speaker of the poem's reliance on broad generalizations, Mario sets up an opportunity to introduce hypothetical examples that will test the logic of the poem.*

> *However, he does not fully capitalize on this opportunity by generating concrete instances in which the speaker's logic would not apply.*

In this poem, Kipling makes a claim that overcoming setbacks is always easy. I disagree with this statement. I disagree because depending on the situation it can be either easy or hard to overcome it. The speaker in the poem only talks about emotional setbacks. Physical setbacks can be a lot harder to deal with. Not everyone is strong enough to bounce back.

Moving Forward

- We need to work with students on generating examples from everyday experience to test claims against.

- Mario reads the poem very literally. We need to give students some direct instruction on the figurative nature of poems as a way to comment on a topic.

Applying What We've Learned to a Literary Argument

LESSON PLAN

Purpose/Learning Intentions: Apply what we have learned about argumentative reasoning to writing a literary argument, while recognizing that authors take different positions on major issues. Practice considering how authors and texts relate to one another.

Length: 45 minutes

Materials Needed

- A class set of Handout 15.1, "Mother to Son" by Langston Hughes

Lesson Steps

Step 1: Link the upcoming lesson to the lesson on "If."

- Recall that we learned that in both greeting cards and poetry, we need to consider three key questions:

  → Who is the speaker?

  → Who is the audience?

  → What is the occasion?

- Note that that means doing more than identifying someone's role. That is, it's one thing to say that the speaker is a parent, but they should imagine just *what kind* of parent. How old? From what circumstances? and so on.

- Explain that they will get additional practice in answering those questions today.

Step 2: Provide a mini-lesson on metaphor.

- Write the expression "Life is just a bowl of cherries" on the board. Ask students what that means. After a brief discussion, make a couple

UNIT CONTEXT:

What makes someone resilient? The poem in this lesson, "Mother to Son" by Langston Hughes, should be taught after Kipling's "If."

LESSON BACKGROUND:

As we noted in the background to the lesson on Kipling's "If," we want students to see themselves as authorized to disagree with what characters, speakers, and authors say or think. One way to foster that authority is to have students read texts through which authors take up positions that compete with or contradict each other. If authors and texts are arguing with one another, then students will see that your agenda is not to have them all agree with an author or with each other.

Part of what comes with developing authority as a reader of literary texts is being able to generate thematic interpretations that move beyond simple platitudes. Our experiences with students have shown us that they are often too quick

(Continued)

to conclude that the content of a poem can be summed up by an easy cliché. While there is some value to being able to succinctly state a central idea of a poem, we want our students to attend to the nuances of the piece first. This lesson, like the previous, is also designed to promote complex reasoning about what may appear to be a rather straightforward poem.

We also noted that we want to teach transferable reading skills whenever we can. We do that in this lesson by focusing on metaphor to provide students with strategies that they can bring to their readings of other literary texts.

of changes to the sentences, for example, "Life is a walk down a dark alley" or "Life is not a day at the beach."

- Briefly discuss the alternative sentences and how they suggest a different idea about life.

- Ask students to complete one of the following two sentences:

  Life is _____.

  Life is not _____.

- Ask four or five students to write their sentences on the board. Ask all students to rank them from the one that is most positive about life to the one that is most negative. Have a brief discussion about why. So, for example, a student commenting on "Life is just a bowl of cherries" might say, "Well, cherries are delicious and sweet, so the statement means that life is sweet too." Or a student commenting on "Life is a walk down a dark alley" might say, "Bad things happen in dark alleys. They're scary. And even if something bad doesn't happen, you're expecting it to. So that statement means that you have to be really worried about bad things happening in life."

- Explain that the kinds of comparison that they just made are called metaphors. If you think it's appropriate for your students, you could also explain that metaphors have two parts:

  1. The *tenor*, or the subject one is trying to describe (in this case life)
  2. The *vehicle*, the things whose attributes you are ascribing to the subject (in this case, the bowl of cherries, the walk down the alley, and so on)

- Explain that they should be alert for metaphors as they read the poem.

Step 3: Have a whole-class discussion of the poem.

- Distribute Handout 15.1.

- Read the poem aloud.

- Note that the title of the poem provides the beginnings of answers to two of the three key questions, "Who is the speaker?" and "Who is the audience?"

- Remind students that you want them to think about detailed answers to the above questions. Ask them to discuss the following questions in pairs:

  → How old is each?

  → What do you know about what their lives have been like?

  → What can you say about what kind of person they are?

- After 10 minutes or so, reconvene the class and ask students to share their ideas. As they do, use the Toulmin probes to get students to elaborate their ideas.

- As students respond, identify the metaphors they draw on in making their judgments. For example, students might draw on the metaphor of the crystal stair to make a claim about the circumstances the speaker of the poem has faced throughout her life and say, "Crystal is fancy. So the speaker hasn't had a fancy life." Another might chime in and say, "Stairs take you straight up higher. I'm thinking that she had ups and downs or something."

- Brainstorm possible occasions for this poem (e.g., high school or college graduation, just having been fired from a job).

- Ask students to explain which they think is most likely. Once again, use the Toulmin probes to get students to elaborate their ideas.

- Give students 3 minutes or so to complete the scales on the handout.

- While they are doing so, draw each of the scales on the board or some chart paper.

- Tally responses by asking, "How many put it all the way over to *within* yourself?" As you did in the "If" lesson, move point by point until you have moved through all of the scale points. Ask students to explain their ratings, making sure to use the Toulmin questions "Where do you stand? What makes you say so? So what?"

- Lead a similar discussion with Scale 2.

Step 4: Have students use the sentence frame and complete their paragraphs.

- Explain that one of the things they need to do at the beginning of all of their written arguments is to situate the reader even when the reader is their teacher or a classmate.

- Explain that the example sentence frames on Handout 15.1 will help them do that, but that they are on their own in supporting their claim. Encourage students to ask themselves the Toulmin questions to help them write.

- As students plan and write, circulate. If needed, refer to the scales or use the Toulmin probes to help students compose.

Step 5: Have students share their writing in pairs.

- Divide students in pairs to share what they have written.

- Have partners ask these questions of their partner's paper:

  → Is the claim clearly stated and both defensible and controversial?

  → Do the data provide a safe starting point? Are they sufficiently explained so that the audience can understand them?

  → Does the author connect the data and claim with a warrant? Does the warrant provide a general principle that applies beyond the specific situation?

Extension: Have students imagine that they are making a movie of the poem and ask them to cast the mother and son. Explain that they can either suggest actresses and actors or that they can find an image of someone they think would be suitable for the role. Have them support their choices.

"Mother to Son" by Langston Hughes

Well, son, I'll tell you:

Life for me ain't been no crystal stair.

It's had tacks in it,

And splinters,

And boards torn up,

And places with no carpet on the floor—

Bare.

But all the time

I'se been a-climbin' on,

And reachin' landin's,

And turnin' corners,

And sometimes goin' in the dark

Where there ain't been no light.

So boy, don't you turn back.

Don't you set down on the steps

'Cause you finds it's kinder hard.

Don't you fall now—

For I'se still goin', honey,

I'se still climbin',

And life for me ain't been no crystal stair.

(Continued)

Scale A: The speaker of the poem believes that resilience primarily comes from

Within yourself   Others around you

Scale B: The speaker of the poem argues that overcoming setbacks is

Always easy   Never easy

Writing Portfolio

In Rudyard Kipling's poem "If," the speaker is a father addressing his son. In "Mother to Son," by Langston Hughes, the speaker is a mother addressing her son. In both poems, the speaker is not the poet himself, but rather a made-up persona through which the poet makes an argument about resilience.

Create a mini-argument in which you form a claim that explains the main difference between these two poets' views of what makes someone resilient. Use the poems as data for your claim. To help you develop your claim, you may want to use one of the following frames:

Langston Hughes, author of _____, believes _____, whereas Rudyard Kipling, author of _____, believes _____.

The poems _____, by _____, and _____, by _____, demonstrate the authors' differing views on resilience. Their differences can be best understood as _____ versus _____.

Langston Hughes, author of "Mother to Son," believes that life will be hard but you can't give up, whereas Rudyard Kipling, author of "If," believes life can get hard but you can ignore it. The poems demonstrate the authors' different views on resilience. Even though they both think bouncing back is never easy, one is from a mother's perspective and the other is from a father's perspective. The father tells the son that maybe one day he may have to overcome a setback. By the mother's perspective, she's telling him that he will have setbacks that he'll have to overcome. She provides her life as an example, telling him that if it happened to her, it will happen to him, but if she was able to overcome it so will he.

> Sasha sets up a comparison rooted in interpretation.

> Here she shifts into a more literal comparison. The importance of the difference she identifies is not made clear.

> She's using data from the poem to build her argument but the connection between the data and the claim is not explicit.

Moving Forward

- When working with literary texts, we need to give students explicit opportunities to practice with literal and figurative responses.

- We may need to provide students with additional instruction on and practice with using explicit warrants to connect data to claims.

Learning the Reader's Rule of Rupture

UNIT CONTEXT:

What makes someone resilient? The lesson could also be used in other contexts, for example, a unit on autobiographies or one built around the essential question "What is the best response to oppression?"

LESSON BACKGROUND:

In our lessons on "If" and "Mother to Son," we displayed two of the central features of our approach to teaching literary texts: creating a context for genuine argumentation and teaching transferable reading skills. We display them in this lesson as well. You'll see how the lesson takes up a genuine question—"What makes someone resilient?"—and how we try to teach a transferable reading skill, in this case a rule of notice. Jeff Wilhelm and Michael Smith have written extensively on teaching rules of notice in *Diving Deep Into Nonfiction* (Wilhelm & Smith, 2017), but in brief, a rule of notice is a shared understanding authors and readers have. For example, we know we're supposed to pay attention

LESSON PLAN

Purpose/Learning Intentions: Apply what you have learned about argumentation to writing a literary argument. Apply the rule of "rupture" to your reading.

Length: Approximately 75 minutes in one block or over two classes

Materials Needed

- A projector to display computer images

- Access to the excerpt "Learning to Read" from *The Autobiography of Malcolm X*. The excerpt begins on page 118 and continues through until page 120. In it, Malcolm X describes the process by which he taught himself to read and circumstances that surrounded his learning. X, M., & Haley, A. (1965). *The autobiography of Malcolm X*. New York, NY: Grove Press.

- A class set of Handout 16.1, "Writing an Argument Based on 'Learning to Read' by Malcolm X"

Lesson Steps

Step 1: Give a mini-lesson on noticing ruptures.

- Explain to students that it's impossible to pay equal attention to everything when we read, so authors count on readers paying more attention to some details than others.

- Display an image that has surprising details. We like Nutri Balance's "Bad Food, Bad Dog" campaign. One of the ads in that campaign features two police inspectors questioning a suspect who is sitting in front of a picture window. Outside the window you see the suspect's dog holding the hand of what we have to presume is the murder victim.

- Ask students what they think they're supposed to notice and why. Students will likely mention the dog right away. Explain that the creators of the ad were counting on our noticing the dog because the image is so surprising. Display other images and ask students to notice what's surprising in them. Note that authors have the same expectation: that their reader will pay special attention to surprises. Explain that you want them to pay special attention to surprises in the next reading.

Step 2: Have a whole-class discussion of "Learning to Read" by Malcolm X.

- Distribute Handout 16.1. Tell students that you want them to mark any sentences they find especially surprising.

- Read the text aloud, pausing to define any words your students might find unfamiliar (e.g., *emulate* or *riffling*).

- Upon completing the reading, ask students what surprising sentences they noticed. Their answers don't really matter; what's important here is to establish that surprises are worth attending to. However, it is likely that they will notice the last sentence in which Malcolm X says that despite being in prison after he learned to read, "I never had been so truly free in my life." Have students discuss what he might have meant by that sentence.

Step 3: Have students complete and discuss the two resilience scales.

- Give students 3 minutes or so to complete the scales.

- While they are doing so, draw each of the scales on the board or some chart paper.

- Tally responses by asking, "How many put it all the way over to Inner Strength?" Move point by point until you have moved through all of the scale points. Ask students to explain their ratings, making sure to use the Toulmin questions "Where do you stand? What makes you say so? So what?"

- Lead a similar discussion with Scale 2.

Step 4: Have students complete the ranking activity.

- Give students 3 minutes or so to complete the ranking activity,

- Divide the class into groups of four or five to discuss their rankings. Explain that their discussion is preparation for the writing they will be doing.

- As always, as groups are discussing circulate. Use the Toulmin probes to generate elaborated discussion as needed.

Step 5: Have students work individually with the paragraph frame to draft an argument.

to titles, especially when the language of the title shows up in the body of the text. (a "call to attention"). In this lesson, we focus on another rule of notice, a "rupture," that is, a surprise of some sort. As experienced readers, we know we're supposed to notice and think hard about ruptures. Less experienced readers may not know this.

We also want to highlight another aspect of our approach in this lesson: posing problems in lieu of (or in addition to) asking questions. Research paints a pretty dismal picture of the quality of classroom discussions. Applebee, Langer, Nystrand, and Gamoran (2003), for example, found classrooms featured virtually no open discussion while Elizabeth, Ross Anderson, Snow, and Selman (2012) reported that students typically respond politely to teacher questions without considering or acknowledging the thoughts, comments, or ideas of their classmates. One of the difficulties we've experienced in trying to generate high-quality discussions is that questions often aren't very useful tools for generating them. Too often, we've found, they cue single answers, and our students respond politely rather than as engaged readers. Instead of thinking of ourselves as question askers, we've tried more and more to think of ourselves as problem posers. Semantic differential scales are one kind of problem. So too are ranking activities. You'll see both of those tools in operation in this lesson.

Step 6: Divide students in pairs to share what they have written.

- Once again, have partners ask these questions of their partner's paper:

  → Is the claim clearly stated and both defensible and controversial?

  → Do the data provide a safe starting point? Are they sufficiently explained so that the audience can understand them?

  → Does the author connect the data and claim with a warrant? Does the warrant provide a general principle that applied beyond the specific situation?

- Circulate among the pair to make sure that students are giving their partner's paper a critical read.

Extension: Have students find other examples of print material or texts in which the creator cues the need to pay attention through the use of a rupture.

Writing an Argument Based on "Learning to Read" by Malcolm X

Scale A: Based on his account of learning to read, Malcolm X would most likely argue that resilience is primarily a product of

Inner strength   External support

Scale B: Malcolm X implies that the ability to overcome setbacks can be found in

Any situation   Only certain situations

Writing Portfolio

Rank the following factors according to how significantly you think they contributed to Malcolm X's ability to overcome the setbacks he faced in his life prior to and during his time in prison. Place a "1" next to the most significant factor.

_____ His relationship with Elijah Muhammad

_____ His skill as a hustler

_____ Copying pages from the dictionary

_____ Participating in weekly debates

_____ Learning about the world from books

Now, write a short argumentative paragraph in which you explain and justify your rankings.

The most significant factor that contributed to Malcolm X's resilience was _____. Another significant factor was _____. _____ and _____, on the other hand, were not as significant. As I see it, there is evidence to suggest that the most important factors that contribute to resilience are _____ and _____. For instance, [*here you need to provide evidence to support your first factor*]. This shows that [*now, provide a warrant to show how your evidence connects to your understanding of resilience*]. Another kind of evidence worth considering is [*here you need to provide a second, different kind of evidence to support your second factor*]. This shows that [*now, provide a warrant to show how your evidence connects to your understanding of resilience*].

online resources ⟵ Available for download at **resources.corwin.com/writersofargument**

Nakia successfully draws her claims directly from the ranking activity.

Here she supports her claims through data from the text.

Providing more data is a good move, especially when considering a reader who may not be familiar with the text.

Nakia's argument is still missing an explicit warrant, although her reasoning implies that Malcolm X's resilience was closely linked to his interpersonal relationships and desire to communicate with others.

The most significant factor that contributed to Malcolm X's resilience was his relationship with Elijah Muhammad. Another significant factor was participating in weekly debates. Copying pages from the dictionary, on the other hand, was not as significant. Malcolm X's resilience was mostly based on his relationship with Elijah Muhammad because he followed Elijah Muhammad's teaching and admired it but he couldn't write back and sound intelligent which frustrated him because he had a lot to say. I think the debates were another thing that contributed to Malcolm X's ability to overcome the setbacks he faced. He admired the intelligence of some of the guys and that led him to read and write and learn. From learning that, that's when he began to understand what was occurring in the black community.

Moving Forward

- Nakia does not fully take up all three of her initial claims. We have to encourage students to explain not just their claims, but also the reasoning behind their counterclaims.

- We have to remind students that even when the underlying logic of their arguments is evident, it is still important to provide explicit warrants.

Applying Argumentative Strategies to Respond to a Well-Known Theory

LESSON PLAN

Purpose/Learning Intentions: Apply argumentative strategies while reading and responding to a well-known theory from the field of psychology.

Length: 90 minutes in one block or two class periods

Materials Needed

- A class set of Handout 17.1, "Erikson's Theory of Social Development"

- A text that adequately summarizes Erikson's work, written at a level appropriate for your students

Lesson Steps

Step 1: Relate this lesson to what has preceded.

- Explain to students that they will be bringing together their understandings of argumentation and the strategies they have developed as readers and writers of arguments as they read and respond to a college-level assignment.

- Explain to them that they will be learning about a well-known theory derived from the work of the psychologist Erik Erikson. Tell them that Erikson was interested in how our social encounters influence who we become as adults in life.

Step 2: Develop background knowledge.

- Ask students to think about an influential experience from their childhood involving some kind of social interaction—with a parent or caregiver, a friend or classmate, etc. Have them share their experiences with a partner and explain why it was influential.

UNIT CONTEXT:

What makes me *me*? This lesson can also work as a stand-alone.

LESSON BACKGROUND:

The next lessons come from a unit we designed specifically for the college-bound seniors in our Pathways program. The unit question "What makes me *me*?" involves examining the constellation of factors that contribute to who we are: our inherited traits; our family and local community; our race, gender, and ethnicity; and our personalities as unique individuals. Throughout this unit, we try to prepare seniors for both the argumentative tasks they will confront as they apply for college, such as the SAT and the application essay, and the kinds of readings and assignments they are likely to encounter in their early-college coursework. Such courses often involve wrestling with complex theories and building a

(Continued)

knowledge base around the seminal work of scholars in many fields. The next two lessons provide students with opportunities to leverage the argumentative strategies they have developed into the kinds of formal, academic tasks they will need to master for success in college.

Erik Erikson's theory of social development is a mainstay in many general education and introductory psychology courses in college. Typically, students in such courses read textbooks that distill the theory into its most salient implications, and the students are often asked to compose written arguments in which they evidence their understanding of both the theory and its implications. Moreover, many colleges prompt students to write personal statements in which they reflect on themselves and their life experiences. Demonstrating knowledge of the work of well-known theorists can help students to compose effective statements that will likely get the attention of the admissions officers who are adjudicating their applications.

Our data for this lesson include a table we generated that summarizes the main stages of Erikson's theory. We suggest that you accompany this table with a reading that you feel is appropriate for your students. Many psychology textbooks include discussions of Erikson's theory, and there are also a number of useful resources available online.

- Poll the class on their responses to the following scale. You can have them copy it from the board and circle their responses, or you can have them vote with their feet as they move to pre-determined spaces in the classroom.

The person we grow up to be is primarily a result of:

- Let students discuss their responses, using Toulmin probes as necessary to direct the discussions.

Step 3: Have students read about Erikson's theory.

- Since the texts being used will vary for this step, we encourage you to decide on a strategy to guide their reading that you feel will be appropriate. Call upon any of the lessons in this book for examples. For example, use the rule of rupture as they read. Develop scales and/or paragraph frames that cue students to key aspects of the text. Make sure you allow opportunities for discussion both during and after the reading.

Step 4: Have a whole-class discussion about Erikson's theory.

- Distribute Handout 17.1.
- Ask students to mark each scale one at a time.
- To get a sense of the whole class, draw each scale on the board and ask how many people marked each scale point. Continue until you have all of the tallies.
- Choose a student who gave a mark near one of the poles of the scale. Use the Toulmin questions to help the student elaborate his or her reasoning.
- Turn to a student who gave a mark near one of the other poles. Once again, use the Toulmin questions to help the student elaborate his or her reasoning.
- Turn to a student who gave a mark near the center. As usual, use the Toulmin questions to help the student elaborate his or her reasoning.
- Continue the discussion in this way for each scale until the energy in the discussion has waned.

Step 5: Have students put their arguments into writing using the prompt on Handout 17.1.

Step 6: Have students work in pairs to respond to each other's work.

- Ask them to circle the claim, that is, the answer to the "Where do you stand?" question, on their partner's work.

- Ask them to put each piece of data, that is, the answer to the "What makes you say so?" question, in brackets.

- Ask them to underline each warrant, that is, the answer to the "So what?" question.

- Have partners discuss what elements of their arguments work best and which ones might need improvement.

Extension: Have students research another theory of human development (e.g., Piaget) and make an argument as to which they find more persuasive.

Erikson's Theory of Social Development

Erik Erikson (1902–1994), a German psychologist, developed one of the most well-known theories of human development. Erikson's theory was based on what he viewed as a series of central conflicts that define various stages of our lives. The conflicts are rooted in our interactions and relationships with others. According to the theory, successfully resolving each conflict results in "virtues," or favorable outcomes. The list below briefly describes each stage and the outcomes that can result when the conflict is resolved favorably.

Stage 1: Trust vs. Mistrust (Ages 0–1)

Infants who receive consistent care are able to trust others and gain a sense of security.

Stage 2: Autonomy vs. Shame and Doubt (Ages 1–3)

Toddlers who are supported and encouraged in their independent choices gain confidence in their ability to adapt to the world.

Stage 3: Initiative vs. Guilt (Ages 3–6)

Children who are given opportunities to assert themselves and exercise their own ingenuity become more comfortable as leaders and decision-makers.

Stage 4: Industry vs. Inferiority (Ages 6–13)

Children whose initiative and ingenuity are reinforced by caregivers and teachers gain confidence in their ability to achieve goals.

Stage 5: Identity vs. Role Confusion (Ages 13–19)

Teenagers who are given opportunities to explore different options about themselves and their potential futures gain a sense of their role in the world.

Stage 6: Intimacy vs. Isolation (Ages 20–30)

Young adults who are able to sustain close friendships and romantic relationships develop a sense of care for others and learn to value commitment.

Stage 7: Generativity vs. Stagnation (Ages 30–60)

Adults who raise their own families, find success in their jobs, and develop close ties to their communities and other organizations develop a sense of themselves as productive members of society.

Stage 8: Ego Integrity vs. Despair (Ages 60+)

Senior citizens who are able to reflect on their own lives with a sense of purpose and accomplishment feel satisfaction and contentment.

Scale A: According to Erikson's theory, children's social development is based on

The same few factors — Many different factors

Scale B: Erikson believed that the first 3 years of life were _____ to later development.

Unimportant — Very important

Scale C: According to Erikson's theory, by the time children reach adolescence, their personalities are primarily a result of

How they were raised — Individual characteristics

Scale D: Erikson would argue that there are _____ paths toward healthy social development.

A few — Many

Writing Portfolio

Based on Erikson's theory, the most important factor that contributes to who we are can be summed up as [*make a claim based on the theory*]. To understand why, one has to know a few things about the theory, such as [*summarize a few data points from the reading*]. Of course, Erikson's theory is only useful if we can agree on certain assumptions about people. One such assumption is [*provide a warrant to explain Erikson's theory*] and I [*agree or disagree*] with this assumption because [*explain*].

online resources ◆ Available for download at **resources.corwin.com/writersofargument**

Based on Erikson's theory, the most important factor that contributes to who we are is the particular way we are raised. To understand why, one has to know a few things about the theory, such as if I was told what to wear instead of getting the option to choose from the age 3–6, I would depend more on mom and dad instead of being independent. Of course, Erikson's theory is only useful if we can agree on certain assumptions about people. One such assumption is that things like trust and autonomy have a lasting impact. I agree with this assumption because if I wasn't able to pick my own clothes when I was young I would depend on my fiancée now.

> Juan's claim is both debatable and defensible.

> Although Juan has an interesting example here, he is too quick to jump to it without clarifying how it illustrates a specific tenet from Erikson's theory. He might have assumed his reader would already be familiar with Erikson's work.

> Juan's warrant clearly connects his claim to his example.

> Juan repeats his example but it is not as strong as he would like it to be here because it oversimplifies the impact of other stages of growth.

Moving Forward

- Practice generating examples that help to illustrate complex theories.
- Work with students to develop criteria for what makes an example effective. Use the peer annotation assignment as a guide.

Bringing Together All of the Elements of Argument: The Minnesota Twins Study

LESSON PLAN

Purpose/Learning Intentions: Practice evaluating data from seminal scientific research in order to compose an argumentative response.

Length: 90 minutes in one block or two class periods

Materials Needed

- A class set of Handout 18.1, "The Minnesota Twins Study"

Lesson Steps

Step 1: Relate this lesson to what has preceded.

- Explain to students that they will be bringing together their understandings of argumentation and the strategies they have developed as readers and writers of arguments as they read and respond to a college-level assignment.

- Explain to students that they will be learning about a well-known research study that set out to understand the role of genetics in determining what makes us who we are.

Step 2: Develop background knowledge.

- Briefly introduce the concept of correlation to students. Explain that correlations measure the relationship between two variables. Things that correlate highly are closely related. However, it is important to note that not all correlations are necessarily *causally* related (an infamous example from education is the correlation between shoe size and reading level!).

- Ask students to brainstorm different things that they think might be highly correlated. Examples might include education and income levels, air temperature and ice cream sales, high school GPA and college GPA, etc.

What makes me *me*? This lesson could also be used as a stand-alone lesson, or in a series of lessons focused on the critical reading of nonfiction.

LESSON BACKGROUND:

As in the previous lesson, we designed this one for our college-bound seniors to give them practice with the kinds of concepts and tasks they will encounter in their early-college coursework. General education courses as well as introductory courses in many disciplines often involve exposing students to seminal scholars and studies that have had a lasting impact on the shared knowledge of the field. In this lesson, students will explore some of the data generated through the landmark studies conducted on identical and fraternal twins by researchers at the University of Minnesota.

In the context of the "What makes me *me*?" unit, this lesson reflects some of the influential work of

(Continued)

LESSON BACKGROUND:
(Continued)

scientists who have sought to understand the role of genetics and inherited traits in determining who we are as adults. By studying over a thousand pairs of twins, many of whom were separated early in life and reared apart, the researchers at the University of Minnesota built a database of compelling findings that support the powerful influence of genetics on many different aspects of us as people: our intelligence, personality, interests, and dispositions.

Lastly, this lesson brings together all of the elements of argument as well as the many strategies for reading and writing we have covered throughout the book. It is meant to model the kinds of academic work students are often expected to carry out independently in college courses by asking them to develop accurate summaries and argumentative responses to composite accounts of well-known research. The data we provide in Handout 18.1 are a very succinct overview of some of the findings from the decades of research carried out by scientists working in the field of twins studies. It includes both a set of summary paragraphs as well as a graph depicting the results of many years of IQ testing. This dataset is designed to model the kind of material many students will encounter in the textbooks they are assigned to read for their college courses.

Step 3: Have a whole-class discussion about students' examples.

- Ask students to share their examples aloud. Use Toulmin probes to prompt students to articulate their reasoning.

- Call on other students to evaluate each example.

Step 4: Have students work in groups to examine the data from Handout 18.1.

- Distribute Handout 18.1, "The Minnesota Twins Study."

- Explain to students that the graph at the top of the page presents a series of correlations.

- Divide the class into five groups.

- Instruct students to read through the three sections of Handout 18.1 and together develop a set of three scales (one for each of the three sections following the graph) that illustrate the argument each section is making. Tell students that the frame they should use to introduce the scale for section 1 is "According to the data in Graph 1, it can be argued that intelligence is primarily influenced by. . . ." Tell students that the frame they should use to introduce the scale for section 2 is "The similarities between Gerald Levey and Mark Newman suggest that the way one lives one's life is primarily influenced by. . . ." (Note: For each of the first two scales one pole will likely be something like "Genetic make-up.") Tell students that the frame that they should use to introduce the scale for section 3 is "The critiques of the Minnesota Twins study make the conclusions of that study. . . ."

Step 5: Create jigsaw groups to share their scales.

- Assign each student in each group a number from 1 to 5. If there are more than five students in a group, start again at number 1 and keep counting off until everyone has a number, 1–5. Depending on the size of your class, you may want to adjust the number of groups so that no single group includes more than five students.

- Reorganize the groups according to the assigned numbers (in this manner, each new group will include at least one student from each previous group).

- One at a time, have students share their scales with their new group. Encourage students to use the Toulmin prompts to question each other's thinking.

- Circulate and monitor the discussions.

Step 6: Have students put their arguments into writing using the prompt on Handout 18.1.

Step 7: Have students work in pairs to respond to each other's work as they did in the previous lesson.

- Ask them to circle the claim, that is, the answer to the "Where do you stand?" question, on their partner's work.

- Ask them to put each piece of data, that is, the answer to the "What makes you say so?" question, in brackets.

- Ask them to underline each warrant, that is, the answer to the "So what?" question.

- Have partners discuss what elements of their arguments work best and which ones might need improvement.

Extension: Have students research a pair of celebrity twins and develop an argument on the extent to which their experience supports the Minnesota twins studies.

The Minnesota Twins Study

IQ Tests by Subject

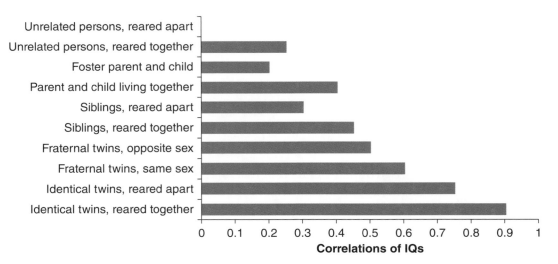

Graph 1: IQ Correlations

The Minnesota Twins Study

In 1979, a scientist named Thomas Bouchard set out to study the similarities and differences between twins—both identical and fraternal—who were separated within the first 6 months of their lives and raised apart from each other. Over the course of 11 years, he and his research team collected data on over 1,500 pairs of twins, as well as over 350 adopted and biological siblings. The data they collected included multiple measures of personality, mental abilities, values, interests, motor skills, reading, spelling, and writing. Additionally, they conducted detailed medical assessments and lengthy interviews with many of their subjects. Many striking similarities were found among individuals who shared the same genetics, even in cases where they were not raised in the same household. In 1990, Bouchard published the results of this study. His work was highly received by scientists in many different disciplines, some of whom saw his work as strong evidence that many of the factors that determine what people are like are rooted in our genetics. The graph above shows the correlations of IQs for the subjects they studied.

A Case Study of Twins

Separated as infants, twins Gerald Levey and Mark Newman grew up to share characteristics ranging from their experiences as firefighters to their tastes in beer. Neither knew of the other's existence until a shared acquaintance brought them together. Upon meeting for the first time each saw his own reflection. They had grown the same mustache and sideburns, and each wore the same glasses. As the brothers talked, they discovered they had more than looks in common. Levey went to college and graduated with a degree in forestry. Newman planned to go to college to study the same subject but opted to work for the city trimming trees. Both worked for a time in supermarkets. Levey had a job installing sprinkler systems. Until relatively recently, Newman had a job installing fire alarms. Both men are bachelors attracted to similar women—"tall, slender, long hair." In addition to being volunteer firefighters, they both share favorite pastimes of hunting, fishing, going to the beach, watching old John Wayne movies and pro wrestling, and eating Chinese food in the wee hours after a night on the town. Both were raised in the Jewish faith but neither is particularly religious. Both men drink only Budweiser beer, holding the can with one pinkie curled underneath and crushing the can when it's empty.

In becoming acquainted, observes Jerry, "we kept making the same remarks at the same time and using the same gestures. It was spooky. . . . He is he and I am I, and we are one."

Arguments Against the Study

Despite its impact, questions have been raised about the reliability of the twins study. For example, separated twins shared the same environment before birth. Researchers are not certain how much this can influence our later development. More importantly, separated identical twins are rarely separated at the moment of birth. The twins in the Minnesota study had on average 5 months together before they were separated. If the first 6 months of life are indeed important, environment could still be contributing to their similar personality traits. Third, after their reunion, the twins averaged nearly 2 years together before they participated in the study. Naturally, the researchers paid special attention to their similarities and may have overlooked important differences to strengthen their findings. Finally, many critics have argued that because most of the twins came from white, middle-class households, their similarities are a result of social and economic advantages rather than shared genetics.

Writing Portfolio

Based on the data collected through the Minnesota Twins Study, one could argue that [make a claim based on the data]. The data support this claim in a number of ways, such as [briefly summarize specific data points to support the claim]. Overall, the study seems to argue that what makes us who we are is [provide a warrant to connect the data to the claim]. However, there are some limitations to the study. Most notably, [briefly summarize one or more arguments against the study].

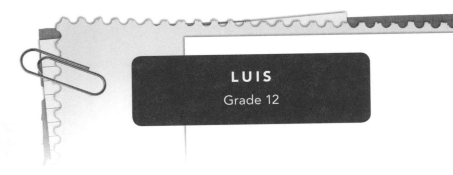

> *In order to reach a wider audience, Luis might elaborate his data by more clearly describing the methods of the study.*

> *Luis's argument includes all of the necessary elements, but it commits very strongly to a single position. Readers will need to know more about the data from which this conclusion is drawn in order to find it convincing.*

Based on the data collected through the Minnesota Twins Study, one could argue that people who are related to each other are going to have many similarities. The data support this claim in a number of ways, such as correlations on IQ tests and similar personality types. Overall, the study seems to argue that what makes us who we are is just the way you're born. However, there are some limitations to the study. Most notably, the researchers may have overlooked a lot of things that were different between people just to get the results they wanted.

Moving Forward

- Luis seems to have a strong understanding of the elements of argument and how they relate to one another.

- Students may need more help providing detailed summaries of the data from which claims are drawn.

Notes

_____

_____

_____

_____

_____

_____

_____

_____

_____

_____

_____

_____

_____

_____

Chapter 7

Putting It All Together:
Applying Argument to Life Choices

One of the things that we've come to realize in our work at the urban comprehensive school at which we taught the lessons we're sharing here is that teachers face a paradoxical challenge. It is our job to prepare students for tomorrow, but we can only do so by engaging them today in issues that matter in the here and now (cf. Smith & Wilhelm, 2002). As we argued in our introductory chapters, the students with whom we work see the academy and academic argumentation as something foreign and distant. We try to bridge the gaps by introducing argumentative reasoning and the writing of arguments through activities that are close to home. Our students were thinking about their college options when we taught this lesson, so we were teaching for tomorrow with materials that matter today.

Should I Choose a 2-Year or 4-Year College?

LESSON PLAN

Purpose/Learning Intentions: Analyze a variety of data and use it to apply what you have learned about argumentation to crafting an everyday argument.

Length: Approximately 90 minutes in one block or over two classes

Materials Needed

- Computer access
- A class set of Handout 19.1, "2-Year or 4-Year?"

Lesson Steps

Step 1: Link the lesson to what has preceded.

- Remind students that they have been developing effective arguments by doing the following:
  - → Making claims that are clearly stated and both defensible and controversial
  - → Offering data that provide a safe starting point and are sufficiently explained so that the audience can understand them
  - → Connecting the data and claim with a warrant that provides a general principle that can be applied beyond the specific situation
- Explain that they'll be applying the skills that they have gained to their analysis of a decision they will all soon be facing: deciding to apply to a 2-year or 4-year college.

Step 2: Develop background knowledge.

- Ask the class to brainstorm what criteria they would use in making the decision. The list should include cost, likelihood of graduation, and

UNIT CONTEXT:

What does it mean to be successful? The lesson could also be used as a stand-alone.

LESSON BACKGROUND:

We want our students to recognize that the skills they are developing are useful both in school and out. One way to engage them in understanding that fact is to have them apply what they have been learning to important life decisions that they will soon be making. In the context in which we were teaching, one of those life decisions was whether to go to a 2- or 4- year college, so it is with that decision we chose to begin.

future benefits. It's likely that it will include other factors as well, for example, convenience.

- Explain that you want students to apply the criteria as they read a variety of different websites that take up this issue.

- Explain that you have developed scales that address three of the criteria, but that they should read also being mindful of the other criteria.

Step 3: Engage students in researching the issue.

- Distribute Handout 19.1. Explain that they will be researching this issue and that they should mark the first three scales on the basis of their research. Leave the fourth scale blank for now.

- Depending on the abilities and experience of your students, you could either have them do internet research on their own, or you could direct them to the sites we used when we taught the lesson:

  → Breakthrough Collaborative, an organization that promotes college access to minority students across the country. Their website provides a wealth of information and can be found at www.breakthroughcollaborative.org

  → The Condition of Education report from the National Center for Education Statistics, which can be found at http://nces.ed.gov/programs/coe.

  → The abstract and tables from Belfield, C. R., & Bailey, T. (2011). The benefits of attending community college: A review of the evidence. *Community College Review, 39*(1), 46–68.

  → The abstract and tables from Marcotte, D. E., Bailey, T., Borkoski, C., & Kienzl, G. S. (2005). The returns of a community college education: Evidence from the National Education Longitudinal Survey. *Educational Evaluation and Policy Analysis, 27*(2), 157–175.

- Circulate as students are working, making sure that they are attending to all the data before they mark the scales.

Step 4: Have small-group discussions of the scales.

- Divide class into six small groups.

- Assign each group one of the first three scales to discuss. Explain that they should discuss how they marked the scales and why. Explain that they do not need to come to a consensus, but if they do not, they need to be able to explain why they could not.

- Circulate as small groups are working. Use Toulmin probes as needed to foster discussion.

Step 5: Have a whole-class discussion of the scales.

- Have groups report. Encourage the rest of the class to ask questions if they have them.

- Ask students to rank independently the three scales in terms of the importance of the criteria. Tell them to group the other criteria that they brainstormed and include them in their ranking.

- As you have done in the other ranking activities, get a sense of the whole by putting a matrix like the following on the board and asking, "How many of you gave this criterion a 1, 2, 3, 4?"

- Choose the criterion about which there is the greatest disagreement. Ask a student who gave it a 1 to explain why. Use the Toulmin probes "What makes you say so?" and "So what?" If students don't articulate a general rule say, "And the general rule is?" to help the student elaborate his or her opinion. As students talk, write ideas to the anchor chart as needed.

> Criteria for choosing
> a college
> _____
> —Can I afford it?
> —Will I graduate? ⎫ All
> —Is it practical? ⎭ one?
> —Is it worth the
>   risk? ↕ are these the same?
> — Good investment?

- Turn to a student who gave the scenario a low ranking and repeat the process. Continue to call on students as long as there is energy in the discussion.

- Repeat the process with the remaining criteria.

	1	2	3	4
Likelihood of graduation				
Annual cost				
Future earnings				
Other				

Step 6: Guide a whole-class discussion of Scale D.

- Give students a minute to mark Scale D on the basis of their research and the class discussion.

- Tally responses by asking, "How many put it all the way over to A *few very specific students?*" Move point by point until you have moved through all of the scale points. Ask students to explain their ratings, making sure to use the Toulmin questions "Where do you stand? What makes you say so? So what?"

Step 7: Have students write their paragraphs.

- Note that all of the classroom discussion should make them well prepared to write.

- Remind them to draw on all the paragraph frames that they have done to craft their argument.

- Circulate as students are writing, providing help as needed.

Step 8: Divide students in pairs to share what they have written.

- Once again, have partners ask these questions of their partner's paper:

  → Is the claim clearly stated and both defensible and controversial?

  → Do the data provide a safe starting point? Are they sufficiently explained so that the audience can understand them?

  → Does the author connect the data and claim with a warrant? Does the warrant provide a general principle that applied beyond the specific situation?

- Circulate among the pairs to make sure that students are giving their partner's paper a critical read.

Extension: Have students write a letter to a friend or family member in which they advise that person what college choice to make.

2-Year or 4-Year?

Scale A: Based on the data you've examined, students who attend a 4-year college are _____ compared to those who attend a 2-year college.

Scale B: Based on the data you've examined, the annual cost of attending a 2-year college is _____ compared to the cost of attending a 4-year college.

Scale C: Based on the data you've examined, getting a degree from a 2-year college means that you will make _____ than someone who graduates from a 4-year college.

Scale D: Based on the data you've examined and the discussion we've had, 2-year colleges are a better option for

On the basis of your analysis of the data, write an argument in which you explain whether a 2-year or 4-year college is better for you. Make sure you state a clear claim, offer sufficient data that provide a safe starting point, and explain how the data connect to the claim.

Available for download at **resources.corwin.com/writersofargument**

> Juan makes a strong claim but he embeds a piece of data in his claim. More importantly, he does not indicate the source of his data.

> He provides strong data here that a reader is likely to stipulate to.

> Juan's sub-claim is a bit controversial.

> While his data for his sub-claim are not as specific as they were for his claim, he makes a reasonable argument.

> It might benefit Juan's argument to add a few details about himself that explain why the cost and time commitment of a 4-year college would be particularly onerous for him.

A two-year college is better for me because it is on average only 35% of the cost of a four-year college. I would also only need two years to start with my career so that would save me 50% of the cost. Also, I could earn a salary while getting my education. A four-year college takes a lot from a person. For one, it takes twice as much time and even then you have to be a full-time student to finish in four years. Also, it costs a lot more money. For me to attend a four-year college, they would have to offer me a big scholarship or lower the tuition cost. If I can spend less and end up in the same career in half of the time, why even think about a four-year college?

Moving Forward

- This is the first task that asked students to collect their own data. We need to work with them on strategies for identifying and sourcing the data they employ in their arguments.

- We need to remind students to make their reasoning clear by separating their claims, data, and warrants.

What Career Has the Best Potential for Me?

LESSON PLAN

Purpose/Learning Intentions: Practice employing argumentative reasoning, while exploring practical career options.

Length: 90 minutes in one block or over two classes

Materials Needed

- Computer access

- Access to Handout 20.1, "Success in the Health Care Industry," either on paper or as a Google Doc

Lesson Steps

Step 1: Link the lesson to what has preceded.

- Remind students that they have been developing effective arguments by making claims that

  → Are clearly stated and both defensible and controversial

  → Offer data that provide a safe starting point and are sufficiently explained so that the audience can understand them

  → Connect the data and claim with a warrant that provides a general principle that can be applied beyond the specific situation

- Explain that they'll be applying the skills that they have gained to an analysis of a decision they will all soon be facing: What career has the best potential for me?

UNIT CONTEXT:

What does it mean to be successful? This lesson can also be used as a stand-alone (see below).

LESSON BACKGROUND:

Like the previous lesson, we wrote this with a concern for our students' immediate lives—their goals, interests, and aspirations. We wanted to give them a context in which they could practice argumentative reasoning, while also gaining insights into their practical plans for the future. We started off by polling the students on their career aspirations and found that a majority of our students were interested in careers in two particular domains: health care and civil service. We developed this lesson around the first of those two, but we encourage you to adapt the tools we provide to careers that match the interests of your students.

We compiled our dataset for this lesson through a two-part process. First, we asked students to rank some

(Continued)

scenarios to come up with their criteria for evaluating a job or career path. You can find these scenarios at the end of the lesson. After some discussion, the students decided that they were most concerned with the following:

1. How much education or training the job required

2. How much money the job paid on average

3. The potential for jobs and advancement within the career path

4. How stressful the job was

5. How much flexibility the job afforded for the pursuit of family and personal interests

With these criteria in place, we guided the students in conducting some internet research to find data for a number of possible jobs. We identified the jobs based on the courses of study offered by colleges in our local area. Again, we want you to think of this lesson as an example that you can adapt to your own students and region.

Step 2: Develop background knowledge.

- Ask class to brainstorm what criteria they would use in making a career decision. As we noted above, our students identified the following: educational requirements, salary, opportunities for advancement, stress level, and flexibility.

- Explain that you want students to apply the criteria as they explore a number of different jobs within a particular field.

- Note that different people will weigh the relative importance of the different criteria in different ways.

Step 3: Engage students in researching the issue.

- See Handout 20.1, "Success in the Health Care Industry," for an example of the tool we used to guide our students in their research. As we explained above, we filled out the first column that identified different careers in the health care field. The other columns were developed as a result of the discussion in Step 2.

- Have students count off by 4. Assign each number two of the careers. Depending on the abilities and experience of your students, you can either have them do internet research on their own, or direct them to specific websites that provide information on the jobs your students want to explore. We've been pleased with the information and layout of Career One Stop (www.careeronestop.org) as a place for students to get started. Then, the Bureau of Labor Statistics (www.bls.gov/ooh) is a good example of a place to find empirical data on many different careers and career paths.

- Circulate as students are working, making sure that they are finding credible information that corresponds to the criteria they have established.

Step 4: Have small groups work together to share their research.

- Create either four or eight small groups depending on the size of the class.

- Have students share the results of the research.

- Circulate as groups are working, making sure that everyone gets the chance to share his or her research.

Step 5: Create jigsaw-style small groups to complete Handout 20.1.

- Assign one member of each of the small groups into a new group in jigsaw fashion so that all eight occupations are covered.

- Explain that group members should share their research so that the group can complete the chart.

- Circulate as small groups are working to check their progress.

Step 6: Have whole-class discussions about the relative importance of the criteria.

- Ask students to work alone to rank the criteria in terms of their importance.

- Have students share out as to how they ranked the criteria and their reasons why. Prompt them with Toulmin probes as necessary.

- Using the table they have compiled, have students apply their ranked criteria to each job, assigning a score or rating based on the extent to which each job meets or does not meet the criteria they have deemed most important to them.

Step 7: Have students write their paragraphs.

- Note that all of the classroom discussion should make them well prepared to write.

- Remind them to draw on all the paragraph frames that they have done to craft their argument.

- Circulate as students are writing, providing help as needed.

Step 8: Divide students in pairs to share what they have written.

- Once again, have partners ask these questions of their partner's paper:

  → Is the claim clearly stated and both defensible and controversial?

  → Do the data provide a safe starting point? Are they sufficiently explained so that the audience can understand them?

  → Does the author connect the data and claim with a warrant? Does the warrant provide a general principle that applied beyond the specific situation?

- Circulate among the pairs to make sure that students are giving their partner's paper a critical read.

Extension: Have students write a cover letter for a hypothetical job posting related to the careers they have examined.

Success in the Health Care Industry

This activity will give you an opportunity to consider your potential to find success in the health care industry. The following dataset includes information for nine of the fastest-growing careers in health care. Each position includes the following elements:

1. A brief description of its duties

2. Educational and licensure requirements

3. The outlook for the future of a job in terms of both job availability as well as opportunities for advancement

4. The general stress level of the job with respect to the complexity of its duties, as well as the level of patient demand

5. The overall flexibility of the job with respect to being able to choose your own hours, perform a variety of duties, and get involved in other aspects of the profession

We've already filled in the first column together. You should fill in the remaining data based on what you've found through your research.

Review the data carefully. Then, compose a paragraph in which you argue for the career you think will be the best path to success.

JOB	DESCRIPTION	EDUCATION REQUIRED	AVERAGE SALARY	OUTLOOK	STRESS	FLEXIBILITY
Physician	A "doctor" in the traditional sense of the word who specializes in a field of medicine such as neurology, pediatrics, or oncology,					
Nurse Practitioner	NPs work in private practices, hospitals, nursing homes, schools, and clinics—they may even make house calls—so their routines and schedules are anything but typical. NPs are very similar to physicians in that they can diagnose illnesses, prescribe medicines, and sometimes serve as primary caregivers.					
Registered Nurse	RNs are the frontline health care workers who monitor patients, administer medicines, chart progress, and attend to many different day-to-day needs.					
Occupational Therapist	Helps people with handicaps and disabilities adapt to the needs of day-to-day life.					
Physician's Assistant	Works under the supervision of a physician to interpret X-rays and blood tests, record patient progress, conduct routine physical exams, and treat a range of ailments.					
Dental Hygienist	Works alongside dentists to clean teeth and provide other forms of preventative care.					
Pharmacist	Handles all aspects of filling prescriptions, monitoring drugs for possible reactions, and advising patients on how to take medications.					
Medical Equipment Technician	Repairs and maintains all types of complex medical machinery, from MRI machines to X-ray equipment.					

Scenarios

DIRECTIONS: Read the following scenarios and *rank* the characters according to how successful they are. Place a "1" next to the character who you think is the most successful, all the way through to a "5" next to the character you think is the least successful.

_____ **Bryan** has always been passionate about computer programming. Throughout his childhood, he spent almost all of his free time practicing how to create games and programs. His efforts paid off when he applied to college because he earned a scholarship from MIT to study in their advanced computer engineering program. During his time at MIT, he created an original program as part of his senior project. The program was designed to help high school students find and apply for college scholarships by organizing many different scholarships into a single database and allowing users to apply easily by creating a profile and uploading their application materials to the site. By the time he graduated from MIT, the program was only half-finished. Bryan really wanted to keep working on the program, but right after he graduated he took a job working for Microsoft. Not only did his new job allow him very little time to work on the program, but when he took the job, he also had to sign a contract stating that he would not develop any programs that might compete with the interests of the company. Now, 5 years have passed, and Bryan has been making good money working for Microsoft, although he often finds his job very boring, and he wishes he had more freedom to pursue his own ideas.

_____ **Janessa** was thrilled to get her job at an international marketing firm because she'd always wanted to travel. Now, she was truly seeing the world. Each month would find her in new cities and new countries. She ate exotic foods made by some of the best chefs in the world; she stayed in luxurious, five-star hotels; she toured famous landmarks, took in beautiful views of mountains and beaches, and met all kinds of people. And through it all, she always enjoyed her job, too. It challenged her without stressing it out, and she found value in the work she was doing. Unfortunately, though, her job also created some problems in other aspects of her life. Her marriage fell apart after only a year. She rarely saw her family on the holidays. She barely knew her nieces and nephews who were growing up fast. And when her father died very suddenly, she regretted having spent so little time with him during the final months of his life. As much as Janessa loved her life, she sometimes wondered if she would be just as happy if she had a job that kept her closer to the people she cared about.

_____ Growing up in west Philly made **Ernesto** decide early on that he wanted to have a good career. The schools he attended weren't the best—they were overcrowded with few resources, and poverty and crime were major issues in the neighborhood. Nevertheless, his tenth-grade science teacher inspired him to want to study medicine and become a doctor. He worked hard through high school to get the grades he needed for college, and he was accepted into the pre-med program at Drexel University. Once he got to college, though, he really started to struggle. Even though his grades from high school were good, he realized that the quality of his classes was rather subpar. He was far behind the other students in his introductory chemistry and biology courses. His academic adviser worried that he wouldn't be able to meet the requirements for pre-med in time to graduate, and getting accepted to a good medical school would be an even greater challenge without a stronger background in math and science. At first, Ernesto took the news hard. He felt like the world had cheated him out of an opportunity. However, soon after, he discovered a program at Drexel designed to prepare students to become occupational therapists. It wasn't quite the same as being a doctor, but the educational requirements were much less steep and the field was growing rapidly.

Ernesto changed his major, completed the program, and in no time found himself working as an OT at Jefferson Hospital. He loved the job. It was hard but rewarding work, and even though he would never make as much money or have as much status as a doctor, he was proud of what he was able to accomplish.

_____ **Rosalie** grew up in the shadow of her older sister, Nora. Nora was top of her class, a star athlete, and she went to college at the University of Pennsylvania. Now, Nora is a lawyer at a top firm where she is quickly rising through the ranks. Rosalie, on the other hand, worked hard through school, but earned mostly average grades. She went to community college and later finished a degree in elementary education at Temple. Now she works as a kindergarten teacher in Philadelphia. Her family is always bragging about Nora's success. Compared to Nora, Rosalie has always felt like her life was a lot less interesting. There certainly wasn't much there to brag about. However, while Nora's career always kept her from settling down, Rosalie now has a husband and two children. Her family is her entire life, and she loves the time she spends with her children. Her husband is a good man with a decent job in construction. They take vacations to the Jersey Shore and they're saving up for a trip to DisneyWorld. Even better still, her family pays a lot more attention to her now because of the kids. Even though the family still likes to brag about Nora's success, deep down in her heart Rosalie thinks she has the best life anyone could ever ask for.

_____ **Marcus** was always a very promising young person. Even a short conversation with him would reveal that he was very intelligent and good with people. He had a natural curiosity for many things, and he would read books on his own just to learn about things that interested him. In school, good grades came easily to him, but he never seemed too eager to challenge himself. He avoided taking the most advanced classes even though his teachers constantly encouraged him to do so. Marcus didn't see the point. He could read and learn about things on his own. After high school, Marcus went to college. It seemed like the thing he was supposed to do. But he didn't enjoy it at all. The classes were boring, and he had no real connection to anything he was learning about. He dropped out after his first semester and started working a series of different jobs: he waited tables at restaurants, sold ads for a website, painted houses, and even worked for a short while as a youth counselor for a neighborhood organization. As the years passed, it seemed like Marcus was always up to something new, moving from city to city and working different jobs. At one point, he went to Europe for a year and lived off the money he made playing poker! Through it all, his friends and family always looked down on him. They thought he had missed his true potential, and they would ask him when he was going to make up his mind and do something with his life. But for Marcus, he already was doing something with his life. The variety of it was the thing he liked the most. He never felt any desire to settle on just one thing to do or one place to live. He liked his life just the way it was, and if other people disapproved, that was just because they didn't understand.

JOB TITLE	DESCRIPTION	EDUCATION	SALARY (AVG.)	OUTLOOK	STRESS	FLEXIBILITY
Physician	A "doctor" in the traditional sense of the word who specializes in a field of medicine such as neurology, pediatrics, or oncology.	Bachelor's degree in biology or pre-med. High GPA needed. High scores on MCAT exam. Five to seven years of post-college education.	$180,000	Growing field with many opportunities for advancement. Some physicians go into research instead of seeing patients.	Very High	Average
Nurse Practitioner	NPs are very similar to physicians in that they can diagnose illnesses, prescribe medicines, and sometimes serve as primary caregivers.	Must first meet all requirements as a registered nurse. Then, must complete 3–5 years of additional schooling and pass additional licensure exams.	$90,000	Growing field that is becoming increasingly more regulated. Therefore, the educational requirements may become more rigorous. Not much room to advance further.	High	Below Average
Registered Nurse	RNs are the frontline health care workers who monitor patients, administer medicines, chart progress, and attend to many different day-to-day needs.	Bachelor's degree in nursing and pass national licensure exam.	$60,000	Highly growing field that is becoming more diverse as some RNs become involved in clinical research. Advancement requires further education and licensure.	High	Average
Occupational Therapist	Help people with handicaps and disabilities adapt to the needs of day-to-day life.	Bachelor's degree, master's degree, licensure exam, and a certain number of hours of field experience.	$75,000	Highly growing field that is slightly diversifying as it becomes more "scientific." Some opportunity for advancement.	Average	Average

JOB TITLE	DESCRIPTION	EDUCATION	SALARY (AVG.)	OUTLOOK	STRESS	FLEXIBILITY
Physician's Assistant	Works under the supervision of a physician to interpret X-rays and blood tests, record patient progress, conduct routine physical exams, and treat a range of ailments.	Bachelor's and master's degree plus supervised clinical training of 100+ hours and national licensure exam.	$90,000	Considered to be one of the fastest-growing professions in the country, while also boasting one of the lowest unemployment rates. Not much room for advancement, though, and PAs are always in the "shadow" of regular physicians.	High	Average
Dental Hygienist	Works alongside dentists to clean teeth and provide other forms of preventative care.	Minimum requirements include an associate's degree and completion of an accredited training program (approx. 330 exist). State certification is also required.	$70,000	Growing field but few opportunities for advancement. Dental hygienists who want to become regular dentists still have to complete all of the normal requirements.	Low	High
Pharmacist	Handles all aspects of filling prescriptions, monitoring drugs for possible reactions, and advising patients on how to take medications.	Bachelor's degree plus 4-years in a Doctor of Pharmacy program. May also involve residencies. State and national licensure exams.	$120,000	Growing field with great opportunities for advancement in both the clinical as well as the business aspects of the field. Advancement usually requires further training and licensure.	Very High	Very Low
Medical Equipment Technician	Repairs and maintains all types of complex medical machinery, from MRI machines to X-ray equipment.	Associate's degree is the minimum to get started. Most positions require continuing education to keep up with new technologies.	$50,000	Growing field that is expected to nearly triple in size over the next 20 years. Opportunities for advancement are usually pretty good, although it can vary depending on the employer.	High	Low

online resources △ Available for download at **resources.corwin.com/writersofargument**

Nikki might connect better with an outside audience if she transforms the language from the data into more descriptive terms.

This warrant may have come too early in her argument.

Nikki's warrant is explicit and connects some of her data to her claim.

The best job for me would be an occupational therapist. It doesn't have high stress or a low flexibility level. I would have time for my family, which is very important to me. Also, it has an average amount of stress. I don't want to be stressed out to the max. An occupational therapist also personally connects to me. My brother is PDD-NOS and he has an occupational therapist who comes to the house. I love the idea that I would be able to help children similar to my brother.

Moving Forward

- Continue to give students practice in organizing their arguments according to the *claim–data–warrant* sequence we have been working with.

- Talk to the students about presenting data in ways that are descriptive and not just expository, such as through illustrative examples.

Notes

_____

_____

_____

_____

_____

_____

_____

_____

_____

_____

_____

_____

_____

_____

Chapter 8

How to Use This Book

You've just seen 20 lessons that exemplify the approach that we are taking to develop our students into effective writers of academic arguments. As we noted in our introductory chapters, we think that this means not only that our students have the skills necessary to craft arguments, but also that they feel that they are prepared to be members of a community of practice. We hope that these lessons have made our approach clear.

But as we noted in our opening chapters, we are well aware that 20 lessons do not make an entire curriculum. Here's a brief summary of what we did to give you a sense of the whole. In each grade, we began with a series of lessons on everyday arguments like the ones you see in Chapter 4. We interspersed the lessons on the elements of argument like those you see in Chapter 5 by embedding them in additional units we developed for each grade. In Grade 11, we built the additional units around these four questions:

- What does it really mean to be smart?
- To what extent am I responsible to others?
- What makes someone resilient?
- To what extent does the media influence our thinking?

In Grade 12, we only had time to work on three additional units as we also worked with students both to complete a required senior project in which they detailed their short-term and long-term goals along with their plan to achieve them, and to apply to colleges. Two units were centered around new questions: "What makes me *me*?" and "What does it mean to be successful?" We once again considered the question "To what extent does the media influence our thinking?" You'll see examples of the lessons we wrote for some of these units throughout the book.

We recognize that we had more curricular freedom than many of you do and that you might not be able to develop your curriculum around these kinds of questions. So we'd like to close by talking about three ways to use the lessons that we have shared that do not require those kinds of inquiry units.

Using the Lessons Directly

We think that the lessons are ready for you to teach, and we would encourage you to do so. Our suggestions would be to teach the first six lessons, the ones that focus on everyday argumentation, as close to the beginning of the school year as possible and to teach them as a group. Doing so will set the stage for a class in which genuine argumentation is a fact of life, something that's all too rare in the schools we have visited. Doing so will also introduce the elements of Toulmin's model and will prepare students to use the three Toulmin prompts. You could also teach the next six lessons, two on each of Toulmin's three major elements, at the beginning of the school year, but if you can't because you have other curricular demands, we'd suggest teaching them toward the beginning of the year in other units of study. It seems to us to make the most sense to teach them in pairs on consecutive days.

We'd suggest using the other lessons in one of two ways. You might consider doing them in the context of the reading that you are doing. Even if you don't develop a full-blown unit around an essential question, these lessons could enrich the work you do with any text that shares their conceptual focus. For example, Lessons 13–15 all focus on resilience in some way or another. They would be great companions to any reading or set of readings that takes up that issue. We could imagine using them with a wide range of texts, for example, Walter Dean Myers's *The Beast*, or the autobiography *I Am Malala*. All of the lesson focus explicitly on argumentation, so they would be excellent introductions to work you are doing with nonfiction argumentative texts, from *The Federalist Papers* to Thoreau's "Civil Disobedience" to essays written about controversial current events.

The second way to use the lessons would be to intersperse them throughout the year as stand-alone lessons to provide focused practice and review. For example, the lessons would be great way to get your students back into the argumentative groove after a break. They could also provide an excellent and instructive change of pace after finishing one long anchor text before moving on to the next.

Using the Tools

However you decide to use the lessons themselves, we strongly encourage you to use the tools we've discussed in all of the work that you do. The Toulmin probes—Where do you stand? What makes you say so? So what?—operationalize complex understandings. They provide the basis for the internal dialogues in which students should engage when they compose. Using them consistently will keep the culture of argumentation alive in your classroom and in your students' minds when composing arguments elsewhere. We also encourage you to regularly use the transferable reading tools that we provided. The three questions we asked about the poems in Lesson 14 are useful in thinking about any poem and noticing ruptures, the focus of Lesson 16, is an important strategy when reading any kind of text.

> We think that the lessons are ready for you to teach, and we would encourage you to do so.

However you decide
to use the lessons
themselves, we strongly
encourage you to use the
tools we've discussed
in all of the work
that you do.

The scenarios we composed as gateway activities (Hillocks, 1995) provide data that require students to think hard about the issues you want them to consider. We've found that they are great good fun to write, as we noted in Chapter 4. The key to writing them is to understand what makes an issue complex. Say for example, you want to design a gateway activity to introduce *Romeo and Juliet* that engages students in developing criteria for evaluating the quality of a love relationship. What makes that a complex issue? Well, it doesn't take long to think about relationships that we've seen (or had). Is passion crucial even if it's sometime destructive? Is comfort and friendship key even if a spark is lacking? Say you want students to think about what makes a good parent in preparation for evaluating Atticus's parenting in *To Kill a Mockingbird*. Is it how a kid turns out, regardless of how that happens? How involved is too involved? Is quality time or regular time more important? Once you ask those questions, composing a complex little narrative becomes pretty easy. The last question, for example, gave rise to this little scene:

> Julie is an eighth-grader. Her parents got divorced when she was 6. For 7 years she spent about the same amount of time with each of them, but three years ago, her dad moved to California, all the way across the country from her. He had a great job opportunity and he said that the lifestyle there suited him. These days Julie spends every other Christmas vacation and three weeks each summer with him. He calls every week, but it's hard to talk. He has trouble keeping track of current friends and classes. A couple of times when Julie faced a really big decision she called and her dad was really helpful. She knows he'll help her decide what college to go to. Somehow he senses what's best for her. But she wishes he were more interested in the day-to-day details of her life.

Once you've developed a scene, you can use the semantic differential scale tool to focus kids' response. In this case the poles might be good parent/bad parent. If you compose multiple scenes, we suggest asking students to rank them as we did throughout our lessons. Semantic differential scales are wonderfully versatile. They are central to most of the lessons we write. When you use them, you'll see how they focus students' attention on crucial aspects of texts. They support the culture of genuine inquiry because by their very nature they encourage multiple responses. And multiple responses provide the necessity for argumentative reasoning.

Our students write as part of every lesson, often with the support of paragraph frames. One of our favorite quotes about the teaching of reading or literature comes from Margaret Meek (1983) who argues that our central job is to share the "list of secret things that all accomplished readers know, yet never talk about" (cited in Thomson, 1987, p. 109). We think the same holds true for the teaching of writing. We need to share what we know. Our focus has been to help students engage in academic reasoning, but unless they can put their reasoning into writing, it will do them no good, at least not in school. The paragraph frames provide a way to do just that. We've shared a number of examples, but hope that you will develop your own as well. All you need to do is write in response to an assignment that you give and identify the structures you want to encourage your students to try on for size. In his dissertation work, Jon-Philip found that over time, many students took up the frames and made them their own. If you use frames regularly, we think you'll see the same results.

Using Our Lessons as Templates

Finally, we hope that you'll use the lessons we created as templates in creating your own. After all, there are plenty of other everyday arguments that are worth having beyond those we share here. Your students may need more lessons focusing explicitly on the different elements of Toulmin's model than we provide. There are other careers to examine beyond those in the health care field, other theorists worth considering beyond Erik Erikson, other issues to delve into beyond resilience. We hope that the variety of activities we provide; the way we combine speaking, listening, reading, and writing; and our mix of whole-class and various kinds of group discussions are generative as you design additional lessons that help your students develop into successful and engaged writers of academic arguments.

Finally, we hope that you'll use the lessons we created as templates in creating your own.

References

Applebee, A. N. (1996). *Curriculum as conversation: Transforming traditions of teaching and learning.* Chicago, IL: University of Chicago Press.

Applebee, A. N., Langer, J., Nystrand, A. M., & Gamoran, A. (2003). Discussion-based approaches to developing understanding: Classroom instruction and student performance in middle and high school English. *American Educational Research Journal, 40,* 685–730.

Belfield, C. R., & Bailey, T. (2011). The benefits of attending community college: A review of the evidence. *Community College Review, 39*(1), 46–68.

Clark, A. M., Anderson, R. C., Kuo, L. J., Kim, I. H., Archodidou, A., & Nguyen-Jahiel, K. (2003). Collaborative reasoning: Expanding ways for children to talk and think in school. *Educational Psychology Review, 15*(2), 181–198.

Cohen, J. (1992). A power primer. *Psychological Bulletin, 112*(1), 155.

Elizabeth, T., Ross Anderson, T. L., Snow, E. H., & Selman, R. (2012). Academic discussions: An analysis of instructional discourse and an argument for an integrative assessment framework. *American Educational Research Journal, 49,* 1214–1250.

Graff, G., & Birkenstein, C. (2010). *They say/I say: The moves that matter in academic writing.* New York, NY: W. W. Norton & Company.

Hagler, D. A., & Brem, S. K. (2008). Reaching agreement: The structure & pragmatics of critical care nurses' informal argument. *Contemporary Educational Psychology, 33*(3), 403–424.

Herrnstein, R. J., & Murray, C. (1994). *Bell curve: Intelligence and class structure in American life.* New York, NY: Simon and Schuster.

Hillocks, G., Jr. (1995). *Teaching writing as reflective practice.* New York, NY: Teachers College Press.

Hillocks, G., Jr. (2010). Teaching argument for critical thinking and writing: An introduction. *English Journal, 99*(6), 24–32.

Imbrenda, J. P. (in press). Developing academic literacy: Breakthroughs and barriers in a college access intervention. *Research in the Teaching of English.*

Hosseini, K. (2003). *The kite runner.* New York: Penguin.

Imbrenda, J. P. (2016). The blackbird whistling or just after? Vygotsky's tool and sign as an analytic for writing. *Written Communication, 33*(1), 68–91.

Kennedy, B., & Funk, C. (2015). Many Americans are skeptical about research on climate change and GM foods. Pew Research Center. Retrieved from http://www.pewresearch.org/fact-tank/2016/12/05/many-americans-are-skeptical-about-scientific-research-on-climate-and-gm-foods/ft_16-12-05_climate_gmfoods_understanding/

Lave, J., & Wenger, E. (1991). *Situated learning: Legitimate peripheral participation.* New York, NY: Cambridge University Press.

Marcotte, D. E., Bailey, T., Borkoski, C., & Kienzl, G. S. (2005). The returns of a community college education: Evidence from the National Education Longitudinal Survey. *Educational Evaluation and Policy Analysis, 27*(2), 157–175.

National Center for Education Statistics. (2012). *The nation's report card: Writing 2011.* Washington, DC: Institute of Education Sciences, U.S. Department of Education.

Newell, G. E., Beach, R., Smith, J., & Van Der Heide, J. (2011). Teaching and learning argumentative reading and writing: A review of research. *Reading Research Quarterly, 46*(3), 273–304.

Nussbaum, E. M. (2008). Collaborative discourse, argumentation, and learning: Preface and literature review. *Contemporary Educational Psychology, 33*(3), 345–359.

Osgood, C. E., Suci, G., & Tannenbaum, P. (1957). *The measurement of meaning.* Champaign, IL: University of Illinois Press.

Rabinowitz, P., & Smith, M. W. (1998). *Authorizing readers: Resistance and respect in the teaching of literature.* New York, NY: Teachers College Press.

Schneider, J. (2014). *From the ivory tower to the schoolhouse: How scholarship becomes knowledge in education.* Cambridge, MA: Harvard University Press.

Smith, M. W. (2007). Boys and writing. In R. Kent & T. Newkirk (Eds.) *Teaching the neglected "R": Rethinking writing instruction in secondary classrooms* (pp. 243–253). Portsmouth, NH: Heinemann.

Smith, M. W., Wilhelm, J., & Fredricksen, J. (2012). *Oh yeah: Putting argument to work both in school and out.* Portsmouth, NH: Heinemann.

Smith, M. W., & Wilhelm, J. D. (2002). *Reading don't fix no Chevys: Literacy in the lives of young men.* Portsmouth, NH: Heinemann.

Stein, N. L., & Albro, E. R. (2001). The origins and nature of arguments: Studies in conflict understanding, emotion, and negotiation. *Discourse Processes, 32*(2–3), 113–133.

Thomson, J. (1987). *Understanding teenagers' reading: Reading processes and the teaching of literature.* Melbourne, Australia: Methuen.

Toulmin, S. E. (1958). *The uses of argument.* New York, NY: Cambridge University Press.

X, M., & Haley, A. (1965). *The autobiography of Malcolm X.* New York, NY: Grove Press.

Vygotsky, L. S. (1987). Thinking and speech. In R. Reiber & A. Carton (Eds.) & N. Minick (Trans.), *The collected works of L. S. Vygotsky: Vol. 1: Problems of general psychology* (pp. 39–285). New York, NY: Plenum Press.

Wilhelm, J., & Smith, M. W. (2017). *Diving deep into nonfiction: Transferable tools for reading any nonfiction text.* Thousand Oaks, CA: Corwin.

Index

Notes

_____

_____

_____

_____

_____

_____

_____

_____

_____

_____

_____

_____

_____

_____

Notes

CORWIN LITERACY

BECAUSE ALL TEACHERS ARE LEADERS

Nancy Frey, John Hattie, Douglas Fisher

Imagine students who understand their educational goals and monitor their progress. This illuminating book focuses on self-assessment as a springboard for markedly higher levels of student achievement.

M. Colleen Cruz

By flipping the traditional "reading first, writing second" sequence, this innovative book lets you make the most of the writing-to-reading connection via 50 carefully matched lesson pairs.

Berit Gordon

Discover how to transform your classroom into a vibrant reading environment. This groundbreaking book combines the benefits of classic literature with the motivational power of choice reading.

Patty McGee

Patty McGee helps you transform student writers by showing you what to do to build tone, trust, motivation, and choice into your daily lessons, conferences, and revision suggestions.

Leslie Blauman

Teaching Evidence-Based Writing: Fiction and *Nonfiction* help you educate students on how to do their best analytical writing about fiction and nonfiction. Whether annotating a text or writing a paragraph, an essay, or response on a test, your students will know how to support their thinking.

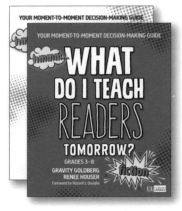

Gravity Goldberg, Renee Houser

With *What Do I Teach Readers Tomorrow? Fiction* and *Nonfiction*, discover how to move your readers forward with in-class, actionable formative assessment in just minutes a day with a proven 4-step process and lots of next-step resources.

800-233-9936

A SAGE Publishing Company

Helping educators make the greatest impact

CORWIN HAS ONE MISSION: to enhance education through intentional professional learning.

We build long-term relationships with our authors, educators, clients, and associations who partner with us to develop and continuously improve the best evidence-based practices that establish and support lifelong learning.

Solutions you want. Experts you trust. Results you need.